D0971759

THE GOLD STANDARD

AUTHOR'S NOTE

The Gold Standard is a satire of life in Hollywood and the peculiar business of show business. Some celebrities' names and real entities and places are mentioned in this book to provide an illusion of verisimilitude. All such real names are used fictitiously. And all names of people in Ari's imaginary past—schoolmates, clients, and friends—are completely made up.

THE GOLD STANDARD

CONTENTS

CONTENTS

INTRODUCTION

My first meeting in Hollywood was with a man named Chaim Roth. Not the character Hyman Roth from *The Godfather*, but a 310-pound Jew who was just as powerful. Chaim had started a record label in 1965, the year I was born, when he was twenty-one years old. I don't remember if he discovered the Beatles or the Monkees or if he came up with the term *groupies* during a sweaty tussle with some of the jailbait he stocked on his yacht, *L'Chaim*. Doesn't matter. Fact was, Chaim Roth owned the music business when I arrived in Hollywood in September of 1990.

Chaim had a mansion in Beverly Hills and liked to fly his own plane to another mansion in Palm Springs (how he managed to shimmy his giant ass into the tiny cockpit of a twin-engine Piper Aerostar is beyond me). He'd fly the nine minutes instead of making the two-hour drive because, as it was told to me, Chaim Roth's time was worth more than gold.

My father had an aunt who had a cousin who had a friend who went to school with Chaim's brother's friend or something. At the end of the day we were both members of the chosen tribe, and that was as close as I could come to having a connection in Hollywood back then. Somehow it was enough to get me the meeting.

INTRODUCTION

Fresh out of law school with my JD/MBA, two hundred grand in student loans, and the 1979 Toyota Corolla that my grandfather left me in his will, I drove to LA with the one suit I owned, prepared to make, as my father would say, a lasting impression on Mr. Roth.

Roth had a fancy office near the water in Santa Monica. The parking fee in his garage was more expensive than the suit I was wearing. The meeting was set for 8 a.m. and, not wanting to risk being late, I checked in with the receptionist at 7:30.

"Ari Gold for Chaim Roth."

I felt important. I was there to see the boss.

"You're early."

I nodded.

"He's usually late."

I felt less important.

The receptionist was a pretty redhead named Caroline. Growing up in Milwaukee she dreamed of being an actress, but after five years of Hollywood disappointment and a couple of amateur "art films," she was on the verge of giving up and heading back to Wisconsin, where she could once again be the prettiest, most talented girl in town. A girl who would never again have to perform fellatio while a director screamed at her, "Trust me, this is going to be the next *Carnal Knowledge*!"

When I told Caroline that I was new in town, she responded with a closed-mouth half-smile that said, *I hope you last six months, then head back to whatever shithole you're from with nothing but a herpes sore to remind you of what a miserable fucking place this is when you fail.*

7:45.

I flipped through a *Hollywood Reporter*. *Goodfellas* was number one at the box office, and there was a big article about Sylvester Stallone's impressive growth as an artist between *Rocky IV* and *Rocky V.* The author compared him to Paul Newman. I thought Dennis Miller was more on target when he said Sly's acting had less range than a Daisy air rifle.

Caroline asked if I needed some water. I said sure and almost spit it out when stinging bubbles hit my tongue. It was the first time I had ever had sparkling water.

Caroline cracked a smile.

9:30.

I'd watched half the office come and go, most sneering at the overdressed kid in the lobby. No one in the record biz wore a suit. Thanks, Dad.

10:30.

Roth finally rolled in, cigar in his mouth, still wearing his golf spikes and yapping on one of those ten-pound-brick cell phones. He covered the receiver with his doughy hand and whispered to Caroline, loud enough for the beach vagrants to hear, that he was on the phone with Madonna.

10:40.

I looked to Caroline for some guidance because not only had Roth not acknowledged me but he had also spent the last ten minutes prepping a bagel while stuffing his face with lobster salad (flown in from Sable's New York at sixty dollars a pound—worth it!) and talking shit about how grunge music would never catch on and he was one hundred percent certain that the dirtballs in Nirvana would be back to selling weed by November.

Chomp chomp chomp. Mayo and lobster that I wouldn't be able to afford for years was flying like his mouth was a goddamn wood chipper as he talked. Disgusting.

10:50.

Twenty-five years later I go nuts when I think back to how that prick made me wait for three hours, but at the time I brushed off the disrespect. In my mind, I was just like Charlie Sheen in *Wall Street*, waiting all day outside Gordon Gekko's office. All I needed was five minutes to impress the guy and then he would immediately kick-start my inevitable ascent to the top of the Hollywood sign. Unfortunately, Chaim was no Gordon Gekko and I didn't get five minutes.

"Mr. Roth will see you now." Suddenly, Caroline was cheerful and accommodating. Roth, meanwhile, continued feeding his fat face a few feet away like I didn't exist.

"Come with me."

Following Caroline down the hall, I couldn't help but notice the perfect shape and buoyancy of her ass (which I would slap repeatedly while banging her in a bathroom stall at the Brown Derby a few months later) and it reinvigorated me. I was certain that I was about to have a life-changing meeting. Caroline deposited me in Roth's cavernous office and scampered back to her desk.

"Take a seat." Roth bellowed as he entered his office, wiping at a stain on his massive polo.

Chaim's office was plastered with gold records and industry awards, along with framed photos of him partying with the biggest acts of the day—poolside with Bell Biv DeVoe, red carpet with Guns N' Roses, courtside at the NBA All-Star Game with Vanilla Ice.

"So, what do you want to do with your life?"

I was startled by the complete omission of small talk but tried not to show it. Fact was, I knew exactly what I wanted to do—I wanted to be an agent—but I didn't want to seem abrasive or presumptuous, so I hedged.

"Well, sir, I'm not totally certain—"

He cut me off midsentence and started sifting through the messages on his desk.

"Come back when you are."

I was stunned. I was hurt. A million thoughts rushed through my head. My father's deep voice rang in my head: *Remember, Ari, always take the high road.*

I painted scenarios. I'll figure out what I want and Roth will see me again, open up the heavens, and let me fuck all the virgins in Hollywood, three at a time.

I heard my father again: *Take rejection with the same class you accept approval, Ari.*

Roth must have been shocked that I was still sitting there. He raised his eyebrows.

"Who sent you here again?"

My father's words kept coming: *Be a mensch, Ari, always.*

"You know what?" I said. I could feel the words forming deep inside, the words that would help set me on the path. "Fuck you!"

"Excuse me?" Chaim was now staring at me full on.

"Fuck you!!!!"

I jumped up, knocked Bobby McFerrin's "Don't Worry, Be Happy" Grammy off Chaim's desk, and just charged out, my father's voice now shouting in my head, *Noooo!* As Roth yelled out for Caroline to call security as he followed me down the hall, I felt a surge of adrenaline that made my dick hard. Roth was seething, nostrils flared, like a wounded buffalo poised to charge. I'll admit I was terrified as Roth screamed obscenity-laced threats and promises, but at the same time I felt a strange sense of power. As the elevator doors closed, I gave him the finger.

I knew at that moment that I was not my father. That wouldn't be the last time I cleared off some asshole's desk, and I was already looking forward to the next time. I was gonna fuck people up in this town.

While driving back from Santa Monica to the two-bedroom apartment I shared with Andrew Shue and two JAPs named Debbie from Long Island, I made myself two promises: I would not stop working until I was in a position to make Chaim Roth feel as small as I felt in his waiting room, and never again would I contemplate not being direct. Chaim Roth gave me a gift that morning in Santa Monica. He gave me a target. And in 2013, after I purchased his record label out of bankruptcy, I sent him a handwritten thank-you note along with a signed photograph of me sitting in his old office, eating from a vat of lobster salad under a shiny new GOLD RECORDS banner.

I would love to tell you that my success in Hollywood was fueled completely by passion and creativity instead of aggression and ambition, but that would be a lie, and this book is about uncensored honesty. I want my children to read this when they're older and apply the principles to their own careers. I want them to understand why I had to miss some of their recitals and basketball games in order to stay late at the office or attend important networking events at the Playboy Mansion. I want them to understand what separates winners and losers in life and what it means to build an empire and protect your crown.

The following are my rules to rule by.

You're welcome.

PART I

VISION

RULE #1

You Don't Have Any Power Until You Have All the Power

"I'm not a businessman, I'm a business, man."

—Jay Z

When people ask me what business I'm in, I borrow words from my man Jay Z: "I'm not a businessman, I'm a business, man."

My clients are movie stars, athletes, business authors, restaurateurs, cartoon dogs, and dead rock stars. I can pick up my phone right now and call thirteen current heads of state and they will pick up. When Seth Rogen wanted to kill Kim Jong-un, who do you think he called first? I own at least two percent of every social network worth visiting. I have the green light to kill a $200 million movie or a Kodiak bear if I feel like it, and four Nobel Prize winners did the chicken dance at my son's bar mitzvah. It took me a long time to get to the top of the food chain, and my journey began in earnest when I learned what is, perhaps, the most important rule of success: *You don't have any power until you have all the power.*

My wakeup call came in January of 1990, in an auditorium at the University of Michigan, where I was getting my JD/MBA. At the time, I was ambitious and eager, but I was also sloppy. I didn't understand that every aspect of my life, from my wardrobe to my wallet, had to be in sync in order for me to matter. Don't get me wrong, I was top of my class and I slayed a ton of ass, but I also wore Birkenstocks in public, rocked a Jewfro and a Hootie and the Blowfish goatee, and had enough body fat to make finding my dick difficult. Unacceptable.

I had attended a number of speaker panels during my time in grad school and always walked out unsatisfied. This panel was different. For starters, it began late, despite the fact that the first two panelists arrived early. Jim Bennington was a VP of corporate strategy for IBM and a total middle-management douche who sported a comb-over like Christian Bale in *American Hustle*. Janet Williams worked for the US transportation secretary and had been a key lieutenant in President George H. W. Bush's election effort. Her bright blue suit had shoulder pads that made her look like the kicker for the Detroit Lions.

Janet and Jim had to wait in their seats like assholes for twenty minutes until the third panelist arrived. And what an arrival it was. The third guy strode up on stage like a panther, decked out like James Bond. He was shouting at the top of his lungs into his massive mobile phone, and for a full three minutes he stood on the stage and proceeded to ruin whoever was on the other end, completely ignoring the four hundred people in the audience, let alone the two robots on stage.

"You have three seconds to wake the fuck up or I'll have

Whitney walk off *The Bodyguard* and you can see if you can get the mom from *The Cosby Show* to replace her. I'd love to see if Claire Huxtable can sell records."

The whole place was captivated. The girl sitting next to me started biting her lip and shifting in her seat, as though this guy's aura was making her moist. Finally, Bond closed the phone, sat down, and said "Let's get this started. I've gotta be on a plane in fifty-five minutes." Badass.

His name was Quinn McBride and he was a talent agent at CAA in Los Angeles. Up to that point, I always assumed that when grad school ended, I would go to New York or Chicago, work for GE or some big law firm, and then spend the next thirty years padding my 401k. But those mundane dreams were incinerated five seconds into that panel. Janet and Jim had carved out nice little careers for themselves, but it was evident that McBride was the only one on that stage with power. At one point during the program, he got into a heated argument with the other two panelists about whether he, Quinn McBride, was more powerful than the president of the United States. The mere fact that the others engaged in the debate and felt the need to defend their positions (Janet Williams worked for Bush!) reinforced McBride's superiority. Twenty-five years later, I have no problem defending McBride's argument myself.

The president can't eat a hamburger or get a hand job without the press jumping down his throat. Power is not defined by one's position, but rather by one's ability to enact change on a whim. The president can't always use his power because of congressional cock blocks. I, on the other hand, routinely move billions of dollars around the world, construct and topple empires, and shape international culture, and I do it all without having to take shit from anyone.

Presidents are not afforded the luxury of discretion, which is why they don't truly max out their power potential until they become ex-presidents. Nobody on the planet wields as much power as a former president of the United States. Ex-presidents of the United States don't need congressional approval to combat the world's problems (they just call me). Ex-presidents are also able to cash in on the strongest personal brand on the planet by giving speeches around the world to companies run by men and women who crave power but will never attain it.

Most Fortune 500 CEOs don't have real power because, at the end of the day, they are controlled by the products they push. Spitting on a sandwich and buffing your sack on it at a fast-food restaurant are child's play compared to what some of my clients have done. I've had clients make sex tapes with teenagers and terrorists, but my brand never suffers. In most cases, in fact, my brand grew with each scandal. Such is the nature of my core business, in which publicity is king and power is attained not by moving product but by moving people.

Fifteen minutes into the panel, McBride dropped the line after which this chapter is named: "You don't have any power until you have all the power." The douche and the kicker scrunched up their faces, but neither dared challenge the validity of the statement. Only the animals at the top of the food chain control their destiny, McBride said. Only the lion is certain of his invincibility. Everyone else walks through the jungle scared that, at any moment, a more powerful beast could jump out from behind a tree and rip out his throat. Today, I am happy to report that I fear no beast. I am too feared, too revered, and far too diversified for any individual or organization to threaten my station, regardless of whether I'm sitting in Beverly Hills or lounging poolside outside a villa in Italy (as I am right now).

The panel was way too short. I didn't want McBride to stop talking. He was unlike any other speaker we had ever had before—uncensored, unfiltered, and brutally honest. When the program ended, McBride got a standing ovation even though he didn't stick around to acknowledge the crowd. He pulled the huge cell phone out of his bag as he walked off the stage.

"What the fuck do you know about age-appropriate casting? You put Ian Ziering on *90210*, and he has grandkids."

He didn't miss a beat, and I was committed to following in his footsteps.

By the time graduation rolled around, I had received several six-figure job offers from companies willing to place me directly into middle management. They dangled great benefits and offered to pay back my student loans. Luckily I recognized that power is never attained by chasing security-driven shortcuts. Power is earned through vision, commitment, and a godlike confidence in knowing that you could do yoga in a maximum security prison shower and no one would so much as glance at your flexible ass.

I have heard a lot of so-called business experts make the claim that in today's fluid economy there is no such thing as a career path. What a load of shit. Most kids today just don't have the patience to chart a career path or the stones to follow through. They don't want to risk failure or start at the bottom. They lack the vision to eschew the six-figure fast track to suburban sedation in favor of chasing the $25K mailroom job that will provide them with the skills it takes to become a predator.

Six months after I moved to Los Angeles, I landed a job in the mailroom of the Terrance McQuewick Agency (TMA). I spent a full year learning the ropes of the Hollywood business and observing the daily routines of a handful of powerful people as I dropped off their mail and delivered their cocaine. I then spent another year as an assistant before being promoted. In those first two years, I answered phones, grabbed coffee, and tracked down my boss's kids when they bailed on rehab. I picked up mistresses from the airport, picked up prescriptions, polished awards, and was forced to stay at the office until I learned how to make an acceptable macchiato. Most of my classmates at Michigan (and Harvard before that) would have considered all of those tasks beneath them. But I knew better. It wasn't about the tasks themselves. It was about proving that I could be the best at every task I touched. Many of my peers at the agency didn't survive those first couple years. I was promoted to junior agent faster than anyone in company history.

I spent the next decade rising through the ranks at the TMA before leaving to start my own agency, Miller/Gold. Less than five years later, I bought TMA and became the undisputed heavyweight champion of Hollywood.

A couple years ago I reached out to Quinn McBride, who at that point was slowing down but still had a sweetheart production deal at Paramount. We had lunch at the Palm, and

McBride pointed out all the women who had used his pole to vault their careers forward before earning the right to have their likenesses painted on the restaurant walls. After laughing about how we shared a few of the same conquests (two high-profile casting directors and a news anchor), I told McBride the story of how he had inspired me to become an agent that day at Michigan decades earlier. He smiled proudly, like Obi-Wan to my Luke.

"You did good, kid. Now don't fuck it up."

For the rest of the lunch we sat across from one another, for the first time, as equals. Man to man. Agent to agent. Jedi to motherfucking Jedi.

■ GOLD NUGGET ■
ALWAYS ANNOUNCE THAT YOUR SPOUSE IS IN THE CAR

If your wife is in the car with you and your phone rings, always answer by saying "my wife is in the car" before engaging in conversation. You never know what the person on the other line is going to say, especially in this town, where everyone swears like pirates and drops sexual innuendos as often as they drop names. The last thing you need is for an executive to say, "I just killed it for you today, Ari. You better chow my slippery box tonight." Obviously it's a joke—at least it usually is in my life—but it will take at least twenty years of couples therapy to undo the damage caused by that momentary flirtation.

RULE #2

Happiness Can't Buy Money

"If you dance on a pole that don't make you a ho."
—Usher

Don't waste time worrying about work/life balance or looking for your best self, sham "secrets," or any other snake oil being pushed by sloppy hippies who have never built a business, let alone a bankroll, or you will wake up twenty years from now poor, pissed off, and primed for a midlife crisis. The cheap beer and strange ass that made you happy at twenty-five won't get you wet at forty-five.

Happiness is a booty call—available and satisfying, but after a few hours you're ready to call an Uber and get back to your real commitments. The idea that someone could or would want to experience uninterrupted happiness over a period of days, let alone years, is ludicrous. Anyone who feels pleasant and bubbly all the time is either mentally disabled or hooked on crack. Money, on the other hand, is steady. You can spend it,

11

invest it, or light a little bit on fire in an intern's ass. Either way, money gets to sleep over.

Money is a resource that makes it easier for you to find your purpose and achieve your goals, not because you are buying happiness but because you are eliminating the desperation that drains happiness and distracts you from your purpose. As my man George Jefferson said, money sure do keep the unhappiness away.

Weak-minded people often try to confuse sedation with happiness, as though the only way to be happy is to piss away the day fly-fishing, sewing cat sweaters, or planning boring dinner parties that make me want to commit Japanese ritual suicide. Retirement isn't a goal; it's a sentence.

I retired once, and I'd rather be forced to rewatch *Unbreakable* than do it again. My retirement lasted six days. I moved to Italy. I painted. I smashed grapes to make my own wine, I planted a vegetable garden, and I made love to my wife morning, noon, and night (and my wife is a yogi who can take it from behind even while facing me). For most people, my retirement setup would seem like a dream come true, but it was a nightmare for me. I woke up sweaty at four o'clock in the morning on day 5 realizing that I hate paint, I hate wine, and I fucking hate vegetables. Thankfully, I still love fucking my wife, but it hit me that if I went back to work I could love fucking her in my office like I did when we were twenty-five. And I could make money. Money money money.

When Bud Fox asked Gordon Gekko, "How many yachts can you water-ski behind?" in *Wall Street,* he was missing the point. (By the way, "Greed Is Good" was the title of my undergraduate thesis in 1986, a year before the movie came out, and my advisor grew up in Stamford with Oliver Stone. I'm just sayin'...)

Buy yachts, stuff cash under your mattress, or give half a million dollars to a German shepherd rescue, like I did, because your daughter cried watching *Rin Tin Tin*. I don't care. Just make sure you have the option. The Wu-Tang Clan said, "Cash rules everything around me," and they were one billion percent correct.

The "money can't buy you happiness" people are the same jerkoffs who coined the word *workaholic*, as though loving what you do for a living is a disease on par with malaria or obesity. More than even loving your family, there is no more important ambition than finding a job that you love. If you don't, you'll reek of self-loathing like a porn star who can't get the box cover, and your family will hate you for it. Loving your work doesn't mean finding a job you can tolerate for eight hours a day, but rather a job that gets you flying out of bed in the morning like a Jack Russell who just had a firecracker stuffed up his ass. Was I ever addicted to my job? Damn right I was. You're fucked if you aren't. You better scratch and claw like a Chilean miner to find a gig worthy of gettin' hooked on. Unlike your hobbies or your spouse, you gotta do your job every day regardless of whether or not it gets you revved up.

I've got more balance in my life now than Cirque Du Soleil, so if you want to follow suit you'd better get started yesterday, because the world is flat and I know thirty million guys named "Kevin" in Bangalore willing to work through the night to ensure that you'll be running their call centers in twenty years. Fight fight fight and get that money money money. 'Cause happiness can't buy even a nickel.

RULE #3

Your Most Important Product Is Heat

"I don't represent talent. I represent temperature."

During my reign commanding the most powerful agency in Hollywood, I regularly interviewed "highly qualified" agent trainee candidates, usually all with prestigious MBAs or law degrees from the best Ivy League cookie cutters in the country. And although I went to Harvard for undergrad, I fucking hate the Ivy League. They're a bunch of elitist pricks who naïvely think waving an expensive piece of paper around paid for by the trust fund their slave-owning ancestors left them is what gets shit done in this world. The way I see it, the Ivy League didn't reject me. I rejected them. That's why I went to Michigan (go Blue!) for my JD/MBA. I could have gone anywhere, but I needed to be back among real people, not picking out which paisley bowtie best matched my boat shoes with the confederacy of blue-blood monkeys lining the halls of the Ivy

League. (And yet, here I am interviewing candidates from Ivy League schools. Yes, I see the irony in it. That's life!)

Despite my preconceived notions of Ivy Leaguers, these allegedly smart, talented, ambitious people had made it through the hellish gauntlet of carefully crafted interview hurdles leading to the final crucible of a face-to-face sit-down with me. Polished young men and women would confidently stride into my office, bedecked with credentials, prepared to wow me with their puerile achievements and accolades. As they handed me their resumes, I always did the exact same thing—threw them in the trash. Then, amid their mounting confusion and terror, I would ask them all one question: "What is the most important thing we sell here?"

I loved watching them twist in the wind as they ransacked their mental database of buzzy business jargon for the right canned textbook reply. They would respond with various grad school babblespeak like, "The most important thing you sell here is…talent" or "people" or "it depends on the fiscal quarter." I'd sit there typing on my BlackBerry for a while before simply shaking my head and saying no.

These buttoned-up overachievers had lived a life where they'd been told by sycophantic mommies and girlfriends that they were winners, so they had no clue what to do. I remember one guy in a Brooks Brothers suit and tie, hair slicked back and reeking of Drakkar Noir like he was Christian Bale in *American Psycho*, who got so flustered, I thought he was going to go into a monologue about how Huey Lewis and the News's early work was a little too New Wave for him, but when their third album, *Sports*, came out in 1983, they really came into their own, commercially and artistically. It was a cheap thrill watching some of these entitled blue bloods squirm, but just because you spent $150K on grad school doesn't mean you got an education.

In all my time asking that interview question, the only person who ever got it right—believe it or not—was a young Asian American named Lloyd. Twenty-two years old. A pudgy Stanford grad who made Liberace seem masculine. He was like the Joey Fatone of a gay South Korean version of NSYNC. "Mr. Gold, the most important thing you sell is *heat*." The correct answer. I had no choice but to hire the little geisha gossip girl right there on the spot. My instincts served me well. That fruity spring roll is now running the TV Department at the Miller/Gold Agency.

Everyone on this planet is a salesman.

Regardless of your gender, occupation, job title, religious affiliation, breast size, IQ, sexual orientation, race, socioeconomic status, blood type, favorite color, ejaculatory distance, or whether you believe the Beatles or the Rolling Stones is the greatest rock band of all time, we're all selling something. I don't care if you're going door to door hawking Girl Scout cookies, peddling your body up and down Eight Mile for some white China smack, or trying to get the cunty hostess at Mozza to seat you on a Thursday without a reservation, you're putting something out into the world in hopes that the world will buy it.

Want someone to like you? You need to sell yourself as a likable person. Want someone to invest in your business? You need to sell them on how you're the man to triple their money. Want someone to have sex with you? You need to sell them on why the pudding in your pop is sweeter than the next guy's.

Heat is a kinetic, volatile, temporary bubble of energy that engulfs whatever it is you're selling—be it a product, a client, even yourself—tipping the scales of attraction in your favor, allowing you to conjure outlandish, outrageous, inconceivable deals that would not be possible under more temperate weather conditions. Heat adds a layer of excitability to the demand side of the equation, triggering buyers to place a disproportionately high value on a product, giving you leverage to demand *more*. Why was Owen Wilson's character in *Zoolander* the highest paid model in the world at the time? Because that Hansel…he's so hot right now! Buzz. Momentum. Juice. It's all the same. You're catching lightning in a bottle and selling it before you hear the thunderclap. Remember, people may eat a steak for the taste, but they buy it for the sizzle.

Heat makes people do crazy things.

Four centuries ago, the whole country of Holland went completely batshit berserk for tulip bulbs. Yes, tulip bulbs. Tulipmania was the first time prices of a speculative asset, in this case—tulips—shot up through the stratosphere. Farms, homes, and families were lost, all because of a flower you send your girlfriend to apologize for sleeping with her sister. Heat is the ephemeral force that compels Midwestern morons to sink their life savings into Beanie Babies, that makes CPAs quit their jobs and spend six months building fallout shelters in their backyards before the Y2K apocalypse, or that lets the latest trainwreck reality star on the cover of *People* convince you to get a Prince Albert after tonguing your asshole in a tattoo parlor outside Juárez.

When dealing with heat, the most important lesson is to keep a cool head. Predicting the weather is more art than science, but you need to develop your own internal Doppler radar system to know when to strike when the temperature is at its peak.

The best time to sell tickets to a volcano is right before it erupts.

Back in my agenting days I used to represent ex–Abercrombie model turned actor Jon Sands. When I found him he was working as a personal trainer up in Vermont, teaching housewives how to be more flexible while their husbands were at work, and taking acting classes at night. He was the stoic, strong and silent type of actor, and I thought he could have a legitimate shot at becoming a movie star. Five years later, when he was coming off his breakout role as high school volleyball superstar Kelly King in the critically acclaimed TV show *Ace High*—a sudser that had teenage girls across America hanging shirtless posters of him on their bedroom walls and calling out his name every time their loofahs brushed against their special tickle place in the shower—he was one of the hottest actors in town.

The heat around him had been building for months, but he wasn't sure if he wanted to stay in TV or try his hand at features. He hadn't had a leading role in a movie at that point in his career, but was getting continual offers to play the second lead or part of an ensemble cast from all over town. These would have been good gigs for any actor, but something about the special brand of heat orbiting Sands at that moment made me think bigger. I had something different in mind.

I'd been tracking a couple of massive, $200 million feature projects at two different studios, each inching their way closer to production. Each movie had suffered significant casting setbacks. Each film desperately needed the perfect piece of talent to upshift it from a blinking yellow to a solid green light.

Sands was just that guy.

The first movie was at Disney, a traditional sword-and-sandals epic with a twist—the whole thing took place on a faraway planet. Okay, sure. It was called *The Space Farmer*, a giant, special effects popcorn movie the studio hoped would launch a new worldwide franchise. It had the potential to put my actor's chiseled mug on T-shirts and lunchboxes all the way from Cleveland to Kuala Lumpur. There was only one small problem. The age of the leading role was early forties. My actor had just turned twenty-two. In most circumstances, that would have been problematic, not to mention that my guy was a TV star who'd never been the lead in a movie, much less carried a summer tentpole on his shoulders. But when you have heat on your side, even the iciest of obstacles can be melted. I convinced Michael Kives, the studio head at Disney and one of the most powerful of his day, that aging the character down made more sense, dramatically and thematically, and that if he cast my client in the part, not only would he be bringing in young men who wanted to see my guy mow down an alien army with a farmer's hoe, he'd get young women who wanted to see him greased up and flexing like Magic Mike in a loincloth, as well.

As my old friend producer Bob Ryan used to say, "Is that something you might be interested in?"

Turns out he was. He cast my client that day.

As my movie star client Vinnie Chase's lesser known actor brother, Johnny Chase, likes to say every time he gets some six's phone number, "Victory!"

Not only had I gotten the character changed, I'd slid my actor in before any other agencies could toss their pathetic hats in the rings. The only thing better than getting a win for one of your clients is simultaneously cock blocking someone else's.

But I wasn't done yet. I didn't want just the one movie. I wanted them both.

The minute it was announced in the trades that my client was starring in the Disney project, I picked up the phone and called Universal, where the other $200 million film was picking up steam. This second project, a war movie set at sea called *Periscope*, also had a twist—instead of fighting one another, the human race was battling underwater zombies. (Why not? It's not my job to do the creative, just to collect the paychecks.) My goal was to use the heat my client had from booking one summer tentpole and roll it into getting him a second. Always double down on heat.

The second studio head, a conservative woman, highly regarded and excellent at her job, was going to be a tougher nut to crack; she couldn't be charmed with swagger or bullshit—she was all business, all the time. I needed to make her see why this would be a smart hire for her bottom line. She was going to put up all kind of walls; I had to find the right grappling hook to scale them.

When I pitched her the idea of Sands in the starring role—
a first lieutenant on one of the warships—she laughed.

"Your client has hair down to his shoulders," she said. "I
can't even envision him as a marine, much less leading a sub-
marine full of them."

"It's called a haircut," I responded. "People will flock to the
movie just to see his new 'do. We'll auction his locks off in a
promotional charity tie-in; it'll be great."

"Who's going to buy a volleyball player commanding a bat-
talion of Marines against a zombie uprising?"

"What do you think, he was the waterboy? He's been playing a star striker the last four years," I said. "Maybe they didn't
have men's volleyball at the boarding school you went to, but
strikers are leaders of men. If he can take a ragtag group of
Montana high schoolers to the state volleyball championship
four years in a row, then he can lead a chorus line of marines to
light up E.T.'s unwelcome ass."

"But there's the Disney thing..."

"Disney made twice the amount of money Universal did
last year. Take a play from their book and cast him before
someone else does."

"Yeah, but we need to shoot in June."

"Perfect! The Disney show shoots March to May. Come
June first, my client will walk on set, reporting for duty without missing a beat."

"The summer release dates are too close together. A two-
month buffer isn't enough. I can't have the Disney movie can-
nibalizing mine."

"He'll be so hot after *The Space Farmer*—which will be *huge*—hits theaters, audiences will be dying for a second helping. You'll brilliantly swoop in two months later for sloppy seconds, and *Periscope* will generate double the box office gross. Look, they'll go see him fight on the sand because he's a heartthrob, but they'll go see him fight on the sea because by then he's a movie star."

"I'm still unsure…"

As you'll experience, occasions arise in heat-based negotiations where, in order to move someone off center, you'll want to play the dark side of the coin. The dark side of heat is fear. The only thing potentially more powerful than the upside of buying heat is the career crippling downside of passing on it. No one wants to be Ronald Wayne, one of the three co-founders of Apple Computer, along with Steve Jobs and Steve Wozniak, who sold his shares early on in the company for eight hundred dollars and now lives in a mobile home park in Pahrump, Nevada, and probably wonders every morning when he wakes up if today will be the day he finally pulls the trigger.

"We're architecting this kid's career like DiCaprio's," I said. "He's going to do two big movies, back to back, then take a long vacation and bang the new models in this year's Swimsuit Edition. If you don't cast him in this movie, I've got two more at competing studios lined up. So if you're passing, that's on you. I'll look forward to next summer when my guy launches two global franchises and I can tell *Variety* you had the chance to get him but passed because you thought his hair was too long. I'll send you a copy of the article to hang in your new strip mall offices in Mar Vista after Universal doesn't renew the option on your contract. I might even sign it for you, too. Probably be worth something on eBay someday."

When push comes to shove, this is Hollywood, and even the most level-headed, conservative executives are susceptible to the mind-warping distortion field that is heat.

She did the deal.

It's important to keep in mind that Jon Sands was a popular TV actor with dreamy eyes and a hairline that could launch a thousand Pantene commercials, but was untested and unproven in the world of feature films. Yet—because I knew how and when to wield heat, manipulate vapor, fan the smoke—it didn't fucking matter. I was able to create two life-changing deals for a client based solely off a qualitative speculation of his potential. Sure, I had a lot to do with driving up the mercury in the thermometer, but that's my job. Heat is like a Ponzi scheme; you borrow from one deal to pay for another until you either hit it big or get caught by the feds with your pants around your ankles. It's the possibility of what could be versus what is. People in Hollywood mistake potential for a guarantee all the time. That's part of why the churn in this town is so high.

Sometimes you play with fire, you get burned.

So, how did this end for Jon Sands? Did he become an international box office superstar? Did his chiseled face jump-start two new global franchises? Does the world go see his movies solely because he's in them?

Not even fucking close.

Remember the *Hindenburg*? That looks like a five-star luxury cruise in comparison to how these turkeys performed. Both *The Space Farmer* and *Periscope* were spectacular financial and critical catastrophes. Studio regimes changed because of these bombs.

It may sound in the retelling like I was using my client as a pawn, but that couldn't be further from the truth. We made these decisions together. I cared deeply for Jon and believed in his talent. I still do. Hindsight is always 20/20, and these were huge opportunities. Ten times out of ten we'd do the exact same thing.

You can't arrive if you're not on the plane.

At the end of the day, you never know if the market will respond to your product. It's always a guess. Sometimes you have to build a house of cards and throw it off a cliff, hoping it finds a sturdy foundation before it falls apart. Unfortunately, these turds disintegrated in midair before even touching the ground. Dead on arrival. All you can do is utilize heat to hype your product, put it in the best position to succeed, and then leave it up to the gods to decide its fate.

So, why didn't the movies work? Because they were just bad movies. There are too many moving parts to assign blame. It was no one's and everyone's fault. And although Jon ultimately wasn't responsible for their failures, someone had to be the fall guy. In the trial of public perception, he got eviscerated. Now, he will continue to get work as an actor, bit parts in movies and on TV, but he'll never open another summer tentpole movie. Jon Sands will never be a movie star. Consider Oscar-winning actor Cuba Gooding Jr.'s career since *Boat Trip*. Out of commission. After *The Love Guru*, when was the last Mike Myers movie you saw in theaters? I wonder what bowling alley bar Brandon Routh is serving drinks at after *Superman Returns*? One embarrassing public flop will knock your legs out from under you. Two in a row ensures you'll never walk again. Do you know what the opposite of heat is? Failure. Like the plague, it's contagious, and people stay as far away as possible so they don't catch it. The problem with heat is that oftentimes when it cools, you freeze to death. But, hey, my guy had a shot. Two, in fact. And that's more than most people get. And hell, what do I know? Screenwriter William Goldman said it best: "Nobody knows anything." It's true. People love a comeback. Ten years ago who would have thought Robert Downey Jr. would be donning a red iron suit and jump-starting superhero franchises? Who would have thought he'd even be alive?

So ask yourself, how you can use heat in your own life?

■ GOLD NUGGET ■
IGNORE THE SCRIPT

I don't read scripts. It's not my job. My job is to make deals on behalf of my clients. Too many agents waste too much time worrying about the strength of material instead of the strength of their deals. Fact is, scripts can be improved, revived, or resuscitated, but once a deal dies the game is over. You can't move forward if you waste the day looking back through act 1. Not to mention the fact that maintaining objectivity is a vital component of my job. It's much harder to sell a script if you know it blows.

RULE #4

Brand Your GSPOT

"Lady in the street but a freak in the bed."
—Ludacris

When I was at Harvard, I really wanted to fuck an art history major named Samantha Freeman. She was an absolute smoke show, and although she was chock-full-o'-nuts, I was willing to overlook the crazy on behalf of her curious mind and sexual voracity. Problem was, I wasn't the only hunter with my eyes on the prize. My chief competition came from a third-generation legacy on the crew team, Miles Van Kampen (MVK), who may very well have been the Winklevoss twins' creepy Neanderthal uncle. Under normal circumstances, I would not have even considered an inbred blue-blood goon like MVK to be competition in my quest to disrobe Miss Freeman, but despite his underwhelming mental acuity and complete lack of social dexterity, the guy did have one thing going for him: a gigantic cock. His nickname was Tripod, and by all accounts he was hiding a Harley kickstand under his Girbauds. It stood to reason that a budding nymphomaniac like Samantha Freeman would be drawn to such a prodigious member, and although I was packing a pretty powerful weapon myself, I still needed a competitive sexual advantage that emphasized precision over girth.

Enter the G-spot.

A female friend of mine put it out on the street that I knew exactly how to locate and manipulate the mythical erogenous zone and word of my accomplishments soon reached young Miss Freeman. At a bar one night in Cambridge, I described to Samantha in great detail the techniques I used for working the G and ensuring otherworldly orgasmic intensity for my sexual partners.

"Some girls sing, some girls cry," I told her. "It doesn't matter whether the climax lasts thirty seconds or thirty minutes, it's always a beautiful form of self-expression."

Check, please.

Although my methodology wasn't even close to being academically sound, I was the only guy around with a thesis on the subject and therefore the only expert. For the rest of spring semester, Samantha and I tested that thesis extensively, while MVK was left holding his (monstrous) extension.

The moment I founded Miller/Gold, we began conducting yearly brand valuations for our clients. I wanted to quantify the value of each client's brand beyond simply box office receipts and previous salary figures. Specifically, I wanted data that no one else had relating to character, street cred, and on-set intangibles. I wanted to show how my people could enhance the experience and extend the enjoyment of making movies, which is why we began studying the client GSPOT.

GSPOT stands for **G**old stats, **S**treet volume, **P**romised land, the big "**0**," and **T**itillation factor. Over the years we found that our GSPOT was so effective for maximizing each clients' earning potential that I had my assistant, Lloyd, secretly set up a GSPOT analysis for me as well. And if you think that financial autonomy, attractive children, and the view from my Italian infinity pool are things you might be interested in, you should start hunting for your own GSPOT.

Gold Stats. The equations we used to mine for paydirt below the surface of Hollywood laziness were inspired by the movie *Moneyball*, which examines how the Oakland A's changed the game of baseball by implementing advanced statistics for performance instead of simply relying on home runs, batting average, and the subjective sex appeal of a given prospect's girlfriend. My favorite *Moneyball* statistic is WARP, wins above replacement player, which tracks job-specific reliability and value. In Hollywood terms, WARP allows you to look at Kevin James's career and statistically diagnose if he brings actual value to a film or if his movies would perform just as well with a coked-out gorilla playing Paul Blart.

WARP also measures the "little things" baseball players do to help the team, like running bases and hiding steroids. WARP was one of the first statistics I adapted in order to show that my girls and guys were winners even when they were playing supporting roles instead of headlining. Just because Rob Schneider can't carry a movie that doesn't mean he can't build buzz for a picture by creeping out female journalists at an overseas press junket.

Our WARP values were tabulated by analyzing the following:

- *Set Stability Algorithm*—Is my client a calming influence on set, resulting in fewer rehab stints and trips to the abortion clinic for the rest of the cast and crew?
- *Dirt Coefficient*—In the event that our clients are not stabilizing influences, do they at least feed the rumor mill in order to ensure that TMZ has the inside scoop when Christian Bale goes postal on a cinematographer?
- *Second Date Rate*—How often were our clients rehired by directors, producers, and studios? It doesn't matter if their performances warranted the rebooking or if they happened to come across photos of an executive producer soliciting a transgender prostitute in the alley behind Astro Burger. Our stats were all about product over process.

Despite concerns that our methodology wasn't robust enough for academic acceptance, I assured our people that our stats just needed to be sexier than everyone else around us, and while our numbers weren't exactly "baby smooth," we were still a landing strip in a town full of seventies' porn bush.

Street Volume. This is a measure of how often, how loudly, and how casually your name comes up when you're not around. The best way to raise your street volume score is to become an "est." Jen Aniston wasn't just sexy, she was the sexiest. Sacha

Baron Cohen was the funniest, Bill Gates was the richest (I'm workin' on that), Amanda Bynes was the craziest.

I didn't give a shit about "well rounded," because in my business only the extremes get talked about. Jay Z and Beyoncé were the busiest. Renée Zellweger was the saddest. Allen Iverson was the laziest ("Practice?"), but at least he stayed in the conversation. My job as an agent was to convert each client strength into an "est" so I that could sell each person as a premium product. I can always make more money with the smartest, stupidest, purest, or sluttiest than I can with a Renaissance man.

Promised Land. Are there certain environments in which your particular set of skills will warrant more cash?

Stephon Marbury never seemed to fit the NBA mold. He was too introspective, too much of a dreamer. His personality clashed with his coaches, most of whom didn't want their point guard discussing his own greatness during twenty-second timeouts. I was drawn to Steph the moment I saw him slow-rolling his solid gold Benz through the streets of Minneapolis in 1996. He was bumping Wu-Tang with the top down. It was December. The wind chill was twelve below. I was in town to go ice fishing with the Coen brothers, but I ended up spending most of my time with the eccentric Timberwolves rookie from Coney Island.

We stayed friends as Marbury bounced around the league for the next decade, never quite living up to his prodigious potential. Steph grew depressed, blaming himself for underperforming his abilities, but I knew better. The problem was his environment.

"Steph, go to China," I said over lunch at the Madison Square Shake Shack the summer after his last NBA season.

"I don't know, Ari. Boston wants me back."

"For the veteran's minimum. Do you really want to spend another year sitting on the bench between Big Baby and Shelden Williams?"

"Nah, man. Those dudes are always quoting Madea, and Big Baby smells like Forever 21."

"Go to China. It's tailor-made for your talents. I spent a week there on the set of *Crouching Tiger*. The Chinese people take a much more philosophical approach to life. And they also love black dudes with ink."

"All right, Ari. If you say so, I'll do it."

In China, Steph flourished both on the court and off of it, where the public embraced his thoughtfulness, spirituality, and weird catchphrase, "love is love." Furthermore, Steph's Chinese coaches were more than happy to let him share his big-picture thoughts with the rest of his teammates, most of whom didn't understand any English.

As I write this, Marbury has won two Chinese Basketball Association titles, sales of his Starbury shoes have never been higher, he is viewed by the Chinese as a Buddhaesque spiritual figure, and the "love is love" motto is chanted awkwardly in arenas throughout the mainland. As a lifelong basketball fan I'll tell you that I've never seen anything like it, and, to be honest, the whole spiritual angle creeps me out like one of Claire Danes's *Homeland* sex scenes, but as I said before, Marbury is a different type of cat. Or maybe he's a panda.

Naturally, after Steph was named MVP of the CBA finals,

NBA teams started blowing up his phone with offers to return to the states. When Steph turned them all down, some general managers complained that he had lost his competitive fire and that he didn't have the guts to compete on the world's biggest stage. Morons. China has the biggest population in the world, and Stephon Marbury is worshipped there as a spiritual basketball deity. The only American in China more popular than Steph is Colonel Sanders.

The Big "0." Business, like boxing, can be infuriatingly subjective, and the only way to ensure that your star stays bright is to keep your "0" by staying undefeated like my man, Rocky Marciano (49–0). Some fights will be easy, while there will inevitably be opponents who will make like my wife and refuse to go down. The key is that when you find yourself on the business end of some left hooks, you cannot, under any circumstances, let the judges see your pain. Stick out your tongue, fire off a few uppercuts, and take back control of the narrative. Just because you take a beating that doesn't mean your "0" has to go.

Ari Gold clients did not get fired. They occasionally starred in projects that underperformed critically or financially, but under no circumstances would I permit the birth of a narrative suggesting that my products did not perform at a satisfactory level. It was well known around town that any directors stupid enough to try to break my streak would be banished from Hollywood, destined to live out the rest of their days directing middle school productions of *Annie* in their shithole hometowns. Occasionally, however, a brazen upstart or overseas import would work up the courage to defy my Golden rule, and for that they would be punished in spectacular fashion.

Verner Vollstedt was both brazen and foreign. He was also an incompetent German fucktard with a putenschnitzel lodged permanently up his ass. Yet somehow Verner was tapped by John Ellis and Dana Gordon to direct a nine-figure blockbuster called *Smoke Jumpers*, starring none other than my bell cow, Vincent Chase. Unbeknownst to me at the time, Verner hated Vince. Not because Vince wasn't talented, mind you, but because Vince had already broken through as a mainstream star thanks to the international success of *Aquaman*. The insecure Kraut fuck was intimidated by Vince's celebrity.

Verner knew that he couldn't get rid of Vince without cause, so he tried to put my boy in a position to fail. He made Vince do more than seventy takes of the same scene over the course of eight hours, berating my guy in front of the entire cast and crew after each attempt. Had I been on set at the time, Verner Vollstedt would have gotten the Shawshank treatment (emphasis on the "shank"). Vince, however, took the high road and tried to reason with Vollstedt, which only seemed to infuriate the bastard even more until finally he blew his lid and tried to fire my boy in the middle of the fucking workday.

Five hours later, Vollstedt and I were both at the studio pleading our case to Dana and John.

"I'm saddled with an actor that can't do the job." Verner was trying to play it cool. "I've got calls into Leo. He and I worked together on a commercial in Austria."

"He's in Boston right now shooting *Shutter Island*." My cool was genuine.

"I've got calls into other actors as well."

"Like who?"

"Joaquin Phoenix."

"Booked."

"Christian Bale!"

"Booked."

"Shit!" Verner was primed for a toddler-worthy tantrum. I just needed to coax it out of him.

"I've got a call into Pete Berg. He loved the script." I then turned to Dana. "Sign off on Berg, and tell the Kraut to get his passport and get the fuck out."

Verner blew up, spit flying from his mouth as he spewed bilingual insults and stormed out of the room. It was a glorious eruption, but that is not to say there wasn't collateral damage. The unrest prompted the chairman of the studio to look into some numbers, at which point he realized that *Smoke Jumpers* was running behind schedule and over budget. Instead of picking between Vince and Verner, he chose to shut down the entire project.

Had I allowed Vince to get sacked in Big Bear, we could have sent out a press release stating that he had walked off the movie. He also could have banked some of the guaranteed money that I had negotiated into his contract. However, the long-term damage to his reputation—namely, the loss of his objectively undefeated record—would have crippled his career trajectory. As it turned out, *Smoke Jumpers* was the last big film Verner Vollstedt was ever allowed to direct. Vincent Chase, on the other hand, was given his next big movie role on the strength his performance in the unfinished *Smoke Jumpers* footage.

Titillation Factor. In 2014, Hollywood was rocked by a celebrity naked picture hacking scandal, commonly known as the Fappening. Some nerdy perverts stole all the celebrity dick and tit pics, and then uploaded them to spank banks on the deep web. The list of affected celebrities read like a who's who of the A-list, many of whom had gone to great lengths to keep their goods offscreen and offline. It was an appalling criminal breach of personal privacy, and the affected celebrities were rightfully outraged (as were their boyfriends and girlfriends, who had to kiss their long-distance celebrity sexting sessions goodbye). Once the smoke of outrage cleared, however, one couldn't help but notice the positive impact the Fappening had on the star power of the naked celebs involved. From a branding perspective, it was a perfect leak because it confirmed for America that their sweethearts had naughty streaks. As my man Ludacris pointed out a few years back, men want a girl who is a "lady in the street but a freak in the bed." The Fappening showed that several of Hollywood's most consummate professionals had not lost their youthful wild side.

Titillation isn't about putting out a slutty vibe like Xtina, or Ray J. Titillation is about tickling the imagination, planting a sexual seed that grows in the minds of the public but never manifests itself in your work (you hear me, Meg Ryan?). It's about spontaneity, excitement, and energy, and it contributes to the legend of your GSPOT.

RULE #5

Develop an ADA (Attention Deficit Advantage)

*"If you have business to discuss, start discussing.
Because I'm busy with my own business."*

I've always had the ability to get more done in less time than most people. I can accomplish in one hour what it takes the rest of the world an entire day to do. There's an old army slogan from the eighties that goes "we do more before 9 a.m. than most people do all day." I was never a soldier, but if I had been, they'd have to change that last part of the slogan to 7 a.m., because by 9 a.m., I already own your soul. This special ability to fire on multiple cylinders simultaneously is how I can sit here right now overlooking the Amalfi Coast drinking a four-hundred-dollar bottle of Giacomo Conterno Barolo Monfortino typing these words on my MacBook Pro with one hand, texting with Wall Street about an equity financing deal on my BlackBerry with the other, all the while mentally categorizing and visualizing the various pretzel-like positions I'm going to treat Mrs.

Ari to on our balcony over an Italian sunset later this evening. In today's world this gift is a veritable superpower many would slice a man's ear off with a straight razor *Reservoir Dogs*–style to possess.

This powerful facility is a big reason why I've climbed as high up the ladder of life as I have. But would you believe that when I was growing up in Chicago in the seventies, this gift was considered a liability rather than an asset? From a very early age, I vibrated at a higher frequency than most mortals. I possessed a tremendous amount of energy, so much so that people said I was radioactive. I glowed in the fucking dark. I wasn't a bad kid; I just couldn't stop moving, couldn't sit still, needed to ABD—always be doing.

If the rest of the world was waiting in line at the DMV, I already had my license and was clocking 120 miles per hour in a red convertible Ferrari down the Autobahn with a wannabe Swiss pop starlet yodeling on my cock like she was auditioning for a Ricola commercial. At the time we didn't have technologically advanced outlets like PlayStations with twelve-button controllers and millions of hypercolor pixels to light up and occupy the brain. There was no Oculus Rift, no high-def Internet porn, no Casual Encounters section on Craigslist to channel our excess energy into. We had to expunge our pep the old fashioned way—by playing sports, committing random acts of vandalism around town, and jerking off to the women's underwear section in the JCPenney catalog.

In a way, I'm grateful for that. Born ten years later, I may have never gotten off the couch from playing Mario Kart to become the Master of the Universe I am today.

A good deal of my surplus energy was directed to running my many side businesses. I did all the typical stuff, like having a paper route and shoveling snow in the winter and selling fake raffle tickets for "charity" door to door, but that was when I was younger and dumber and thought business meant doing all the work yourself; it wasn't until I was in high school that I started recruiting, organizing, and managing other kids in the neighborhood to do all the grunt work for me and paying them a small wage for the privilege of working under my umbrella. In many ways I was like the mafia don among kids under eighteen for my and the surrounding two neighborhoods. I was always happy to do favors, but you had to kiss the ring.

But the best business I ever had in my teenage years was one I didn't even think of. It fell in my lap, brought to me exclusively by one of the techie *Star Trek* nerds down the street—a bespectacled waif of a kid named Erik Lindsay, who did my science projects for me in exchange for my protection from bullies who liked to kick the shit out of kids who spoke Klingon as a second language. Erik was a couple years younger than me, and when he wasn't tearing through sci-fi novels and Japanese manga comics, he could be found tooling around with old radios and electronics in his mom's garage. One day after school he stopped me on the street to inform me of a revolutionary new discovery he had made. By tweaking the rotation of a few screws inside his old cable box, he had figured out how to descramble the pay porn channels that would normally be jumbled black-and-white static. You just had to open the box up, readjust the correct combination of screws, and voilà…

tits! I have to imagine this was similar to the moment when Steve Wozniak told Steve Jobs about the personal computer he had built in his garage. I knew it was going to fucking change everything. Together Erik and I went and bought a bunch of old cable boxes for dirt cheap, repurposed them, and sold them to kids all over town for twenty bucks a pop. We made a fucking fortune, at least for teenaged boys. Parents couldn't figure out why all of sudden everyone stopping hanging out on the street sophomore year. It's because they were busy enjoying "me time" with their little box of Gold. Cha-ching!

And while I could always concentrate on new ways to make money, school was always an issue for me.

Like a shark, I have to keep moving to stay alive. In contrast, the whole premise of formalized public education is to sit still all day listening to the monotonous drone of some middle-aged windbag with cheap shoes and a comb-over attempting to justify his existence on this planet by convincing you that the Pythagorean theorem is actually applicable in real life, which even way back then I knew was bullshit. This was counter-intuitive and frustrating for someone way ahead of his time like myself. There were hills to take, battles to win, worlds to conquer, people to metaphorically slaughter, and there I was, shackled to a desk-shaped cell without a view, the birdman of Roosevelt High School but with no bird to talk to. I got in trouble so frequently that my high school principal, Herb, and I were on a first-name basis. I think he secretly got a kick out of when I'd request to see a teacher who pissed me off's W-2 form to see how much taxpayer money was being wasted every year paying him to be incompetent. I sensed that sometimes Herb felt the same way. Most people in charge do.

One afternoon when I was a freshman in high school, my conservative Jewish mother, bless her soul, at her wit's end with my eccentricities and erratic behavior, took me to our family doctor. His name was Dr. Nico Mizrahi, and he had a spindly hirsute mustache reminiscent of the baseball player Rolly Fingers. I will never forget the day he came into that exam room and told me I had...an affliction. A condition. A handicap. Turns out, I was lacking an abundance of a particular neurotransmitter, a chemical in the brain that regulates behavior. According to this quack, I was suffering from "hyperactivity," medically known as ADD. Attention. Deficit. Disorder. As you can imagine, I wasn't particularly fond of the words "deficit" or "disorder." Back then they didn't have special classes or child therapists or any of that kid-glove crap we soften our offspring with today. If you were a problem child, you got Ritalin. Now not only did this white pill-shaped coma lull you into becoming an obedient labradoodle, it sucked away all your verve, your joie de vivre, your special brand of magic. It was the equivalent of Superman taking a daily pill of Kryptonite. For someone who saw the world in widescreen CinemaScope Technicolor, I was suddenly inside Pleasantville (minus Reese Witherspoon's shapely ass in a poodle skirt), and the world was black and white with no fifty shades of gray. I now understood why Jack always threw a conniption fit in *One Flew Over the Cuckoo's Nest* about having to take his meds. I didn't need to be tranquilized. I wasn't some psycho requiring institutionalization. The bad thing about rounding out your corners is that you lose your edge.

Then I came to one of the most profound realizations of my life.

I wasn't too fast.

The rest of the world was too slow.

And so, as I've done so often in my life, I learned to flip an obstacle into a benefit. Instead of attention deficit disorder, I developed what I call an attention deficit *advantage*. I learned to see the condition as a positive, an accelerant that would help me excel, rather than as an impediment that would hold me back. Because I could process and synthesize mass quantities of stimulation and information faster, I could achieve more in a shorter period of time. It sharpened my ability to cut through the noise and get to the heart of the matter.

It wasn't me who needed to slow down; it was everyone else who needed to keep up. My challenge was to shape the world to adapt to me, not the other way around.

Unbeknownst to my family, I stopped taking the Ritalin, thereby creating a secondary opportunity. While the drug turned me into a drooling mannequin, it had the exact opposite effect for people without my chemical imbalance. It worked as an upper and a stimulant, getting my peers high as kites, bouncing them off the walls like amphetamine-spiked Day-Glo pinballs. In other words, it turned them into an imitation version of me in my natural state. And while I would never label myself a drug dealer, I was not above selling or bartering my Ritalin here and there in exchange for cash and favors or under-the-bleacher handjobs from cheerleaders looking for a little more "high" in their high kick.

Remember the Golden Rule: He who has the gold (or in this case, the Ritalin) makes the rules.

You don't need to be medically diagnosed with ADD to develop an attention deficit advantage. It's less a physiological condition and more a framework for approaching your day-to-day life. Like any new habit or system, it requires practice and discipline and repetition—and then one fine day you'll look up and proudly be able to self-diagnose yourself with a scorching case of chronic, incurable, terminal ADA.

Lucky fucking you.

The author F. Scott Fitzgerald once said that the sign of a first-rate intelligence is the ability to hold two opposing ideas in the mind at the same time and still retain the ability to function. Two opposing ideas? Come on, Scott! Take out your tampon! Two?! How about ten! The more the merrier, I say. That's ADA. Now, I happen to have a special affinity for that ol' sport, F. Scott. As most of you know, his classic novella *The Great Gatsby* was adapted by Martin Scorsese into a brilliant film that brought my boy Vinnie Chase's career back from the dead after getting skewed at Cannes for his "catatonic" performance as Pablo Escobar in the titanic independent feature disaster *Medellin*. In the movie he plays Nick Carraway, and he received rave reviews for his "tempered, measured performance." The movie made $37 million in its opening weekend. Not too shabby for an adaptation of a book written almost ninety years ago by a guy who was drunk more than he was sober. First you take a drink, then the drink takes a drink, then the drink takes you . . . all the way to box office gold, bitch!

ADD is for commoners and suckers.

Develop an ADA and take your reward.

There is a classic rule in screenwriting: When writing a scene, come in late and leave early. In a similar fashion, journalists will tell you not to bury the lead. Songwriters teach the catchy aphorism "Don't bore us; get to the chorus." In other words, in whatever it is you're doing, get to the goddamn point.

There is a finite amount of time to get a seemingly infinite amount of work done. Every minute is sacred. Every second lost is a second you can never get back. You only have so much clock in a day . . . a week . . . a year . . . a life to sell and to be sold, too. You need to squeeze as much blood from the rock as possible.

A good heuristic in all your dealings is to be quick, be bright, and be gone.

Some executives like taking long, leisurely lunches at the Ivy. Others feel the need to bullshit about the Lakers in a meeting for ten minutes before transitioning into business. Even more professionals are compelled to chitchat about who the hell knows what on the phone before getting into why they called in the first place. That may be standard operating procedure for the bourgeoisie, but let me assure you, the pleasantries are unnecessary. I'm a Master of the Universe; I don't have time for that shit. And if you want to be like me—which you all do— you don't have time for it either.

Skip the appetizer, Flo. Bring me the main course.

Some people will think you're being rude, or pushy, or short in adopting this outlooks, but pay it no mind. Human beings are highly adaptable by nature; they'll learn. Think about it: If you were to gather all the minutes wasted on insignificant, immaterial yik yak spent throughout the day and add them up, how much misspent time do you think you'd have? One hour? Two hours? Consider the sunk cost on that. It's unacceptable. With the right resources, I could form a coup and take over a small country in two fucking hours! One minute wasted is one minute too much. Guard your time like you would your money. It's essentially the same thing. Don't let other people write checks your precious time has to cash.

Here are a few examples of how having an attention deficit advantage can benefit you in any given workday:

Meetings. Meetings are the bane of my existence. They are, by nature, bloated and cumbersome, yet also a necessary evil. When it comes to meetings, regardless of the topic, your North Star is to keep them as brief as possible. A meeting should never take longer than twenty minutes, at the outside.

One thing I am renowned for throughout the hallowed corridors of Hollywood are my infamous hallway meetings. What's a hallway meeting? Exactly what it sounds like. An exchange that transpires as I'm walking from point A to point B, usually in a hallway. It's a meeting on the move. Whereas most people just walk, I walk *and talk* like I'm doing a season arc on *The West Wing*.

Walking is something I have to do anyway. Might as well get some business done as I do it.

Consider this incontrovertible fact: At some point over the

course of the day, I am going to have to take a piss. It takes me approximately forty-six seconds to walk from my office to the bathroom. That is a forty-six-second one-on-one window I have available to drop knowledge. If you're not easily embarrassed, I can talk, piss, *and* shit at the same time. LBJ famously had hour-long cabinet meetings as he was dropping a deuce on the presidential throne. His closest advisors and aides would stand outside the crapper with the door cracked, scribbling in their notebooks as he pinched one off.

Then there is the walk *back* to my office. Another forty-six-second window.

Additionally, I have to walk to and from my car, and to and from lunch (if I take one), along with several other ad hoc entrances and exits—all opportunities for an on-the-go hallway meeting. If you came to my agency when I was running it, you would have seen people lined up outside my door all day long, hoping to catch me as I walked out of my office for a hallway tête-à-tête. I was like a college professor holding office hours, except you never knew when those hours would be. Like a genital warts outbreak, they would occur randomly and without warning.

Steve Jobs did the same thing. Except he would often take his meetings outside, walking around his neighborhood or doing laps around the Apple building. There is something about physical activity in concert with mental processing that sparks creative ideas and dialogue. The two go hand in hand. I've had multiple epiphanies while giving a woman multiple orgasms. I've come up with solutions to problems while throwing office furniture across the room. When you adopt an attention deficit advantage lifestyle, you always want to be moving. Motion, action, momentum are key. That applies to everything in your life. Meetings are no exception.

Phone Calls. At the height of my reign, I received at least two or three hundred incoming phone calls a day. That's two or three hundred people vying for a sliver of my invaluable time and attention. Imagine a scene from any medieval war movie where a long row of archers stands atop the perimeter of a castle under attack, pulling back and firing an onslaught of flaming arrows upon an invading army. Those thousands of fire-tipped arrows throttling toward earth are incoming phone calls, and if you're not careful, they'll take you out of the game before you even reach the castle gate.

Because phone calls were the single biggest distraction in my life, I developed a sophisticated phone sheet system that— with the aid of my assistants functioning like special ops team in a CIA war room—could track the person, timing, and reason for all phone calls, allowing me to designate an order of importance around which ones to take first, return, ignore, or roll later in the day. The phone sheet is your fluid strategy plan for the day's battle. It needs to provide up-to-the-second data and be updated rigorously.

No phone call should last more than two minutes. If you can't get across what you need to get across in 120 crisp seconds of articulation, then send a text or an email. In fact, only default to a phone call if what you need to express is more pressing, urgent, or delicate than what can be conveyed via a text or an email. (Or if you're going to be talking shit about the president of the United States like Amy Pascal, then call me.) A useful efficiency strategy for propelling calls along is to never say hello when you or the other person picks up the receiver. Just start talking. Dive right in. It lets the guy on the other end of the line know that it isn't a social call. When a commanding officer hails a solider on a two-way radio, do you think he wants to talk about the weather before issuing an order? No. Just go. During non-working business hours feel free to reach out and touch someone and gab as long as your heart desires. My wife and kids are the only exception to this rule. Whenever they call, I answer. They learned an old trick from me; if I don't pick up the first time, they'll just keep calling until I do. But outside of them, you have to treat workdays as sacred. Don't desecrate it by letting unnecessary phone time eat away at the day. E.T. didn't phone home to chitchat. He phoned home to say, "Pick me the fuck up!"

Lunches. Don't do them. They are a massive time suck and will devour the middle part of your day. Especially if you live in Los Angeles. The turnaround of leaving the building, getting in your car, driving to your lunch, valeting, having lunch, then getting your car from valet, driving back to the office, sitting in lunch traffic, and getting back to your desk all told can be a two-hour swing, if you're lucky. Only take lunches when it is absolutely necessary to meet with someone face-to-face in the middle of the day. If the president calls and wants to grab a bite, sure. But if you don't have the power to launch a nuclear assault on another country, or you're not wanting to break bread over a seven-figure deal, or you aren't a Playmate of the Year offering to jerk me off under the table at the Hotel Bel Air using those little slabs of butter, then I probably won't be carving out the midpoint of my day to have lunch. Have an assistant grab you a sandwich and an Orangina and eat at your desk while working. Industry standard lunch is from 1 to 2 p.m. During that time no one will be in their office, but it's always *not* lunch *somewhere* in the world. Use that time to make and return all of your international phone calls. Trust me, work straight through. People who stop and take a break in the middle of a marathon are more likely not to finish than those who don't press the Pause button. Dinner and drinks are different; you need to do those every single night (I'll go over the reason why in another chapter), but when it comes to lunch, well, there's something ironically poetic about talking on the phone to someone of importance with half a sandwich from Nate 'n Al's sticking out of your mouth.

Another benefit to adopting an ADA attitude is it allows you to filter and block out incoming negativity. If tolerated, negativity and pessimism—like crabs on a Porta-Potty the second weekend of Coachella—will fester, spread, and become infectious. Negativity is a corrosive sludge that will seep in, clog, and choke the otherwise quicksilver linings of your synaptic pathways if you let it. Listening to shit leads to shit work. There's a mental price to letting pervasive pessimism permeate your headspace. People love to throw out platitudes like "think positive" or "look on the bright side," but that's not my tempo. I'm talking about recognizing that there are mental obstructions out there in the form of other people's baggage and not allowing them to pull you into a psychological cesspool with floaties.

In the words of my man Ludacris, when it comes to other people's negativity, "Move, bitch, get out the way."

Having an attention deficit advantage not only prevents you from wasting time, it prevents you from wasting mental energy on other people's headaches. You don't have time for anything except what's going to move you forward. Napoleon had an excellent system whereby no one was allowed to come to him with a problem unless they also came to him with three possible solutions to that problem. In addition to ending the French Revolution, Napoleon was the original spin doctor. Through the creation of his own magazine, he was the first modern man to construct and publicize the image he wanted portrayed. The effects of his PR spin doctoring cannot be underestimated in contributing to his political and military success. He wore funny hats, but the man knew how to get things done.

Every day shit's gonna hit the fan. Stuff is gonna happen, and it's gonna be bad. You just don't know when or how bad it's gonna be. As Cherry Valance said in *The Outsiders*, "Things are rough all over." But you have to put shutters on, set a goal, ignore the noise, and just move the fuck forward. All of that noise is a distraction, and if you let it distract you, you'll fail.

Having an attention deficit advantage helps block out the negative so you can win.

Get infected today.

THOSE WHO LOOK BACK SHALL
TURN TO SALT

I hated going to Sunday school as a kid, but I can't deny that there were a few stories that stuck with me beyond my bar mitzvah, one of which was the story of Lot and his hard-headed wife. Quick recap: Lot was the lucky bastard God spared before carpet-bombing Sodom and Gomorrah, the formerly beautiful cities that, like Los Angeles, had been overrun by vanity, laziness, and impenitent sin. When God slipped Lot and his family their get-out-of-jail-free cards, he had only had one rule—don't look back. Don't waste a second thinking about how the members of your bridge club are being charred like churros. Just move on to bigger and better things (and a ton of creepy incest). Lot got the message but, unfortunately, his wife didn't like being told what to do. On the way out of town, she looked back over her shoulder and was promptly turned into a pillar of Morton's.

Two takeaways from this story:

1. If you ever tell your wife that she absolutely cannot do something, she will go out of her way to defy you, regardless of the consequences.
2. Those who look back shall turn to salt.

Always move forward. Every problem you encounter is an opportunity for you to prove that you are Batman in a business suit. When shit goes down and the sheep freeze up, you need to answer the call and start throwing haymakers. Batman doesn't do damage control. Batman does damage. If you drop me down a well, I won't waste energy crying "Why?"

like Nancy Kerrigan after taking a nightstick to the knee. I will tunnel out of there like my grandparents did when they were escaping the Nazis. Eventually there will be a time for reflection, accountability, and divine retribution, but not until you get out of that goddamn hole.

PART II

REPUTATION

RULE #6

Abandon the Generation of Weakness

"Don't worry, just win."

December 25, 2012. *Django Unchained* had unexpectedly opened number one at the box office, hauling in $20 million more than industry projections. When I negotiated Jamie Foxx's contract, I fought for access to the back end, which meant that my guy was to make exponentially more money than if he had simply been paid his standard quote. Our success was in all the trades that morning, and to celebrate my client and I spent the morning at a very public and expensive champagne brunch. By the time I got back to the office, I was feeling invincible and a little buzzed. When I stepped off the elevator with a bottle of Dom Pérignon, the whole office erupted in applause. A young NYU grad named Johnny Diamond worked on the desk of one of our TV agents, who sat about ten feet away from the elevators, and as I was fist-bumping my way toward the conference room, I heard Johnny's boss tell him to run out and buy more champagne. Instinctively Johnny answered, "But that's not my job." The celebration stopped immediately. Full scratch.

I am all for freedom of speech. I have always worked with people who swear like pirates, and politically incorrect insults will never warrant repercussion on one of my ships. That said, there are a couple of phrases for which an immediate execution is always warranted: "That's not my job" and "That's not fair."

As I began to pump the Dom P like a twelve-gauge a mere three feet from Johnny's colorless face, he tried to take the statement back. He continued to plead his case as I sprayed his face and chest like a hate-fucking elephant. I drenched his Nordstrom Rack suit (I would later admonish his boss for allowing him to wear a bowtie) and his disorganized desk. Unfortunately for Johnny, the fact that "that's not my job" was hanging out in his young brain told me that he would never be worth my time. You either get it or you don't.

I have always run my businesses like a mafia don. I look for people who are tough, ambitious, and loyal, and I give them the opportunity to show me that they deserve a spot in the family. Once they get "made" they are looked at as "earners," not employees, and they are evaluated as such. My earners have a lot of freedom, and the perks are endless. When you are backed by the Goldfather, the city is yours for the taking. Reservations and invitations are no longer necessary. Stores will open up just for you. Legs will open up just for you. Most rules that govern the civilian population will no longer apply to you so long as you continue to earn, show respect, and never ever treat your business like a job.

A job is something you do. A business is something you grow. Regardless of the structure of the organization you work for or the position you hold within that organization, your only job, the only task that matters, is growing your business.

As soon as you start thinking of yourself like an entrepreneur and not an employee, all of the subjective metrics like "effort" and "intent" will melt away and you will begin to see the following categories in HD:

Performance Reviews. I am baffled as to why human resources professionals feel compelled to spend days and weeks conducting 360 feedback evaluations and multiphase quarterly reviews with their employees. My employee reviews consist of one question: How is your business doing? Throughout my career, I myself have made sure that I always have a direct and quantitative answer to that core question. I answer in terms of percentage jumps, box office records, and increased Google search results with the word "naked" following my clients' names. As a result, I have never given myself or anyone else I have worked with any reasons to subjectively underestimate my greatness.

Peer Relationships. Trust and friendship nearly cost me my entire career. When I was effectively running TMA as a junior partner, I set up an emergency escape plan should Terrance McQuewick grow threatened by my influence and decide to move against me. I handpicked eight agents with whom I would flee and start a new agency. I trusted these agents. They were my friends. The success of my plan hinged on their ability to keep our arrangement a secret. What I failed to recognize at the time was that in trusting my eight "friends" with my true end game, I was essentially guaranteeing failure. They knew too much, and, while my vision represented a tremendous long-term opportunity for all of us, all it would take is one sloppy divorce for one of my eight buddies to start eyeing the quick money that could be made by selling me out. The following year, when Terrance did in fact move against me, a young agent named Adam Davies, who had recently knocked up a crazy stripper from the Spearmint Rhino, chose the easy out and exposed my plan. His move paralyzed the remaining seven, and I was left holding my dick while being escorted out of the building.

When you start treating your job like your business, you begin to understand the dangers of allowing yourself to get too personal with your colleagues. Power is a limited resource that only a handful of people will ever control. That is not to say that you can't have friends at work, because you need allies for collaboration and insulation. But you should also make sure that loyalty to your friends doesn't get in the way of loyalty to your business. Don't get stuck playing bass in someone else's band. The bassist almost never gets to go solo.

Risk. In 2011, Charlie Sheen and I met at Dan Tana's, an old-school red-booth Italian joint in West Hollywood, and talked about his career over chicken parm. Charlie wasn't a client, but we'd been close ever since we shared an ambulance to Cedars-Sinai courtesy of some bad tuna melts on the set of *Spin City* in 2001. Anyhow, Charlie was freaking out. After almost a decade on *Two and a Half Men*, Charlie felt unsatisfied and frustrated. He wasn't clicking with his boss on the show and he felt like the job itself had grown stale. After a disagreement on the set went public, Charlie was at a crossroads. He was considering apologizing and riding out his contract, but I wouldn't hear it.

"Carlos," I said. "Why the hell would you go back to that show? You don't need the money, and you have managed to attract some shine with this showrunner beef. Now is the time to evolve. Go nuclear, man."

He wasn't sure. "Do you really think it's worth the risk?"

"Risk? Are you kidding? How long will *Two and a Half Men* last? Two, three more seasons? Then what? You spend five years shaking off the stink of your character? Risk would be letting the spotlight dim. Be provocative. Be bold. Shack up with some hookers and reintroduce yourself to the world."

Needless to say, Charlie took my advice and ran with it. He reinvented his image and rejuvenated his relevance by making himself interesting and unpredictable (and drinking a shitload of tiger blood). What the media perceived as a meltdown was all part of a master plan conceived by me. And it worked to perfection. Six months later, he launched a new rocket with *Anger Management*, his third consecutive syndicated sitcom. #Winning.

When most people talk about career risks, they focus on active risk, aka traditionally risky moves like leaving a comfortable corporate gig for a startup or foregoing a salary in order to increase bonus potential. However, when you start thinking about your job as a business, inactive risk is what causes the jock itch. Risk is when you get so comfortable in a given gig that you don't take the time to set up a pipeline of future opportunities, both internally and externally. Forecasting and strategic planning are essential business planning activities. Once you grasp the essential nature of these tasks for career planning, you begin to realize that risk is not about acting on opportunities to catalyze your career, but rather that the real risk is when you fail to project your five- and ten-year revenue goals and subsequently fail to chart a path to those goals. Real risk is when you trust a company or individual to take care of you and fail to leave any live ammo in the chamber.

Fairness. Over the years, I have had to "whack" several colleagues for whining about "fairness." Erin Foster felt it was unfair that a woman with less seniority had been promoted over her. Erin was promptly promoted to the curb. Frankie Quintero thought it was unfair that his transfer from the unscripted department to feature films was denied. When he came back from lunch, he found out that he had been transferred to the custodial staff for two months. To his credit, the guy shut his mouth, cleaned bathrooms for sixty days, and was granted a return to reality (and reality television).

I have no patience for any "fairness"-driven complaints. Life isn't fair, love isn't fair, and as long as we breathe the free air of a capitalistic society, business will never be fair. Thirty years into my career, I have yet to hear a valid "that's not fair" career-related complaint that wasn't related to gender or racial bias. Ninety-nine percent of the time, the people complaining were underachievers that relied on their own lazy standards instead of common sense. They tried to do a good job instead of running a successful business.

■ GOLD NUGGET: ■
KEEP A JOKER IN THE DECK

When I was a kid, my father didn't want me spending a lot of time with my uncle Damien. Damien was my mother's kid brother, and he and my dad could not have been more different. My dad was a white-collar lunch-pail guy. He woke up at 5:53 every morning; threw on a white shirt, blue tie, and black pants; ate two eggs over easy with his coffee, and was out of the house at approximately 7:08. Uncle Damien sometimes slept in a tent.

Damien never had a job and claimed that people who did were suckers. In reality, Damien had a hard time functioning in society because, although arguably brilliant, he was all idea and no execution. His apartment, when he had one, was covered *Beautiful Mind*–style in "big plans" for everything from counting cards to streamlining the harvesting of soybeans. He lived his life from binge to binge, frequently spending fifty-plus hours straight dialed into a given project and then crashing for days at a time before waking up with a new brilliant scheme.

Naturally, most of his ideas were colossal failures, which I learned after investing a large percentage of my bar mitzvah money into his X-rated foreign-language flashcards (though, in his defense, none of my middle school friends will ever forget that *Jūnan* means "flexible" in Japanese). Damien's ideas weren't necessarily bad, they were just—as my father would say—"out there." The world wasn't ready for medicinal meth in 1981, and the IRS didn't give two shits about suggested tax code revisions submitted by a middle-aged Jewish drifter.

I didn't want anything to do with Damien in high school. I had little patience for his schemes after having had my heart broken by several of his failures as a younger kid, not to mention that the last thing you need when you're sixteen is your crazy uncle trying to sell homemade raccoon jerky in the stands of your JV football game. A few years later, however, when I was home from college for Thanksgiving, I had an epiphany.

Harvard has a notoriously shitty party scene, but every now and again the Phoenix Club would bring in a decent band, bus in some talent from BU, and spend some trust fund cash on top-shelf booze. Problem was, freshmen couldn't get inside without a sponsor, and I hadn't had enough time to work my way in. Anyhow, we're sitting around the Thanksgiving table and I start telling my family about this holiday party at Phoenix that I'm dying to go to when I get back. My father wants none of the conversation, of course, because he thinks I should be more focused on my studies, but my mom and my sister start to brainstorm. Every idea they come up with is something I've already thought of—wait for the band and pose as a roadie, get a job with the catering company, etc. We are on the verge of giving up when Damien walks in, two hours late for Thanksgiving dinner.

"Go as a robot dinosaur."

Damien has the floor.

"Not a T. rex, though. That's too predictable. Go as an herbivore. And make sure you light up."

"Nice of you to grace us with your presence, Damien." My father was disgusted by both the conversation and his brother-in-law. I, on the other hand, loved the idea.

"Damien, that's fucking great."

"Don't you ever use that kind of language at your mother's table, Ari Gold!"

I paid no attention to my father. I had too many follow-up questions for my crazy uncle. Long story short, when I got back to Boston I spent a week gathering materials and engineering nerds to build my robot Brontosaurus. Not only did I get into the Phoenix that weekend, but they offered me a membership right before I left the party with a showstopping senior (and future court of appeals justice), who would later demand that I leave the costume on while bending her over the ledge of one of the many idyllic fountains on campus. I'm fairly certain that we were spotted by a security guard, who, after taking in the confusing visual, simply chose not to engage.

Here's the thing about crazy guys like my Uncle Damien: They don't get stuck, and they don't acknowledge rules. In a business setting, their complete disdain for the status quo can be invaluable. I have actually kept Damien on my payroll for the past twenty-five years. I give him twenty grand a year, which is more than enough to bankroll his lifestyle, and once or twice a year I tap him for ridiculous ideas. When I was struggling to get a studio to fund *Lord of the Rings* with Peter Jackson in the late nineties, it was Damien who suggested we shoot all three movies at once, which was a ludicrous suggestion at the time. Similarly, M. Night Shyamalan and I were having lunch with Damien on the Venice Boardwalk in 1994 when, in between bites of fish tacos, he blurted out, "How fucked up would it be if I was dead right now?"

Always keep a joker in the deck.

RULE #7

Either You Know It All or You Blow It All

"You think there's anything in this fucking universe that you know about that I don't know about?"

If I asked you who the most powerful man in America was during the mid-1900s you might throw out a US president like Truman, a military leader like Patton, or a captain of industry like a Rockefeller; but you'd be dead wrong. Ask yourself this question: Who is the man that presidents, military leaders, and captains of industry are afraid of? The answer: the man who knows their secrets. For forty years, that man's name was J. Edgar Hoover. As the director of the FBI, he was the most powerful information monarch in the United States. Back then, the information superhighway—like a ground ball to Bill Buckner's glove—went straight through him. If there was something worth knowing, favorable or damaging, J. Edgar Hoover was sure as shit to know it. Feared by senators, congressmen, and anyone in power with something to lose, Hoover lorded over them, dangling a scythe above their necks in the form of the simple, singsong phrase "I know something you don't know." The ultimate insider, Hoover wielded the FBI as his own private secret police force, digging up dirt on anyone he needed to get over on, dabbling in sex-life scandals and good old-fashioned blackmail, applying pressure to acquire more and more information, bloodthirsty on the quest to be all-knowing, omniscient. J. Edgar Hoover knew that money may build the church, but information is the god that you pray to.

Why am I telling you this?

Because you need to be the J. Edgar Hoover of your own life. (Living with your mom, dressing up in women's clothing, and hiding your homosexuality from the world are optional.)

How?

Exactly like J. Edgar did: by developing your own spy network, by building out your own homegrown FBI.

Inside and outside of Hollywood, I used to have people everywhere. Still do. Sources. Loyalists. Assets. Friendlies. Operatives. Plants. Sleeper agents. Spies. Whatever you want to call them, they are contacts in various positions across a vast network of businesses, industries, and influential posts I track, gathering reconnaissance and relaying information to me. Some hide in plain sight. Others move in the shadows. But I have eyes everywhere. Little birds whisper in my ears. I'm like Varys from *Game of Thrones* except with hair on my head and genitals above my taint. Many of these Ari-ists, as I call them, are people you may not expect me to associate with. Below-the-line folks. Blue-collar types. Interns, aides, gophers. Parking attendants, hostesses, receptionists. If you want to find out what's going on at the palace, you don't talk to the royalty, you talk to the service staff. All of my finks know I repay tenfold those allegiant to furthering my cause. The only thing better than being the king is pleasing him. Of course I don't usually connect with them directly—there exists an intricate relay system—an interlaced nexus of communiqué filtered through trusted lieutenants up to me.

At the height of his power, famed billionaire, and filmmaker, Howard Hughes had one of the most sophisticated spy networks in all of Los Angeles. Employing a staff of more than thirty full-time private investigators, Hughes practically had his own Gestapo, ordering police detectives' phones tapped, city officials' houses cased, spurned starlets and pernicious business rivals followed and photographed. At one point he contracted an outside group of PIs from Orange County to spy on his in-house PIs in Hollywood, convinced his guys were slacking on the job, eating too many hot dogs. Now, remember, this was the 1930s, when law enforcement in LA was a joke, and if you had money and were hip to greasing the right palms, you could get away with almost anything. Nowadays, you gotta be more cloak and dagger about your recon. A ninja flying a stealth SR-71 Blackbird.

Life is not about learning from your failures; it's about learning so you don't fail.

In Hollywood, there are three essential groups where one must have spies in order to reign supreme. In the industry, we call these groups "mafias." There's the assistant mafia. The gay mafia.

And the Jewish mafia. Each mafia operates within different spheres of influence, brandishing separate but equally powerful fire hoses of information. Collectively, these three mafias cover all the power in town; if you look at them as one overlapping Venn diagram of interlaced circles, you want to be the guy sitting shotgun right in the middle.

Let me break them down for you:

The Assistant Mafia. Every powerful person in business has an assistant. Sometimes several. The president of Paramount has seven, one for each day of the week. These assistants have direct access to the power. They're listening on every phone call, sitting in every meeting, privy to calendars and schedules, always invisible and blending in but a fundamental linchpin in power's day-to-day operation. Assistants are the eyes and ears of this industry. They're the eyes and ears of the world, for that matter. I should know, I used to be one. When I started, assistants didn't interact with each other the way they do now. They were tight-lipped, mistrustful, and competitive. But I realized it didn't have to be that way. While divided we were lower than pond scum, the bottom of the Hollywood totem pole. Together we had an unlikely power. If one day every assistant were to get up and walk out the door, and all of the helpless agents, studio executives, and movie producers across town actually had to answer their own phones, the entire infrastructure and value system of the entertainment business would fall like Saddam Hussein's statue after the Battle of Baghdad. We were more forceful united than we were apart. In such, we began sharing information and resources to help one another advance up the ranks. We became like a family. Stronger. We were a mafia.

Now, I'm not going to say that *I* started the assistant mafia. I'll
leave that for the chroniclers of history to decide. But I was there
that day when the tides changed, and networking in Hollywood has never been the same. Bottom line is, assistants all
talk to one another. They're co-conspirators, brothers-in-arms,
banding together like a company of infantry soldiers stationed
on the front line, their only goals to survive the night without
a bullet to the skull and maybe someday move up the ranks
so they can drink better coffee. They share information with
one another the way Orson Welles drinks at an open bar, lib-
erally and with abandon. Like service industry workers on a
Carnival cruise, assistants in Hollywood live together, party
together, and fuck one another on the reg. At some point, many
of them will rise to power and position in their own regard.
The goal is to follow the Big Tobacco model: Get them hooked
while they're young. Get them early enough and they'll be
addicted to your brand of magic their entire lives. At the height
of my power, I had assistants at every single agency, studio, and
production company of merit loyal to me. Many of those people
run Hollywood today.

The Gay Mafia. Like the displaced Jews wandering the
desert, so once were the gays, a lost ship without anywhere to
dock. So God created West Hollywood in Los Angeles—a
neighborhood to homosexuals like what Willy Wonka's choco-
late factory was to fat kids. Hollywood has always been sexu-
ally agnostic, welcoming all varieties; many smart and talented
gay creatives escaped the puritan confines of their Midwestern
upbringing to head west, where the glittering in the Hollywood Hills matched the glittering in their sequins. Go to Rage

or the Abbey on a Saturday night and you're bound to see some heavy entertainment hitters who earlier in the day were closing deals in Armani suits and are now grinding on top of the bar in neon mesh tank tops and magenta eye shadow. Gay men and women are a powerful force in this industry; like assistants, they band together, forming a tribe that collects and shares information. Be a friend to the gay community. Donate to gay causes, attend gay events. Hire as many qualified gay people as you can. I've even made assistants and colleagues *pretend* to be gay to close business. Once you get over all the histrionics and theatrics, they are actually some of the most fun, intuitive people you'll ever meet. More importantly, they are a veritable pipeline of intelligence. Despite how much shit I used to (and still do) give Lloyd, he knew it was all in jest. Like I said to him once, "I can't promise I won't ever make fun of your sexuality again. But I can promise that I'll always apologize for it afterwards."

The Jewish Mafia. Whereas the assistant and gay mafias have more pliant points of entry, the Jewish mafia is a much tougher nut to crack. You can't just walk up to the temple doors and say, "The password is *Fidelio*." This is the kind of club you have to be born into. (Or convert to, but it's not the same.) Most Jews in Hollywood aren't religious, myself included, but we all *pretend* to be—at the bare minimum showing up for high holidays to keep up appearances and exchange information with our other non-practicing kinsmen. Go to temple on Yom Kippur in Beverly Hills and you might as well be at the Golden Globes, there's so much talent there. If you are Jewish, this is the easiest mafia to infiltrate. If you aren't, not to worry. Here's what you do: Learn a few phrases in Hebrew (Rosetta Stone has a great starter course); buy a yarmulke (and keep it in your glove compartment; you never know when you'll pull up next to a Jewish studio head in traffic on a high holiday and will need to throw it on); know that one of the finest pieces of ass on Earth, Natalie Portman, is Jewish; and if ever asked about Mel Gibson, respond by saying that, while you still hold nostalgic affection for *Lethal Weapon* 1 and 2, you ultimately feel compelled to boycott all his movies, and that deep down you suspect, despite his Australian heritage, that he may be a direct descendent of Hitler. Also, when in doubt, always claim to be a quarter Jew on your mother's side; it's enough to get you in the door to amass the information you need. All these other Jews are so scared of being called out for not attending services enough, no one is going to investigate.

If you happen to hit the jackpot and stumble across a gay Jewish assistant, lock that shit down, put a metaphorical ring on it, because you've just found a unicorn and hit the Powerball in the same fucking day. That's an asset that can seamlessly navigate all three mafias, more precious than gold!

Now I don't expect you to build a turnkey information engine like the one I've built overnight. It takes time. But whatever your business is, develop assets as spies inside the striated networks that comprise it. If you work at a big corporation, you need people in accounting and HR and janitorial, across every division and silo, to feed you intel. Use whatever method necessary to gather information, even body parts. Sometimes the sound of information must be precluded by the sound of bras unsnapping and zippers unzipping. Because—and this is important—you never know what piece of information is going to be relevant to you and your objectives.

When I was trying to get Alan Gray at Warner Brothers to hire Vinnie for this Joey Ramone movie and wasn't getting anywhere, Dana Gordon told me that Alan had no intention of making the movie, he only acquired the script as revenge against Vince for not doing *Aquaman 2*. With this information I went back to the producer on the project, Bob Ryan, who hadn't signed the final paperwork yet, to convince him that if he went with Warner on this, the movie was dead. This was a vital piece of information that could have changed the course of my client's career; unfortunately Bob was old and feeble and weak and ended up going with Warner, where, of course, his movie got parked on a shelf and left to collect dust. But the information I received gave me a shot at resurrection. Why did Dana Gordon give me that info? Because I used to sleep with her back in the day. Never underestimate the power of your penis. Sometimes it'll get you in trouble, but sometimes it's a magic fucking wand.

When it comes to information, you want it all. And by any means necessary.

RULE #8

Be Everywhere

*"Playboy Mansion, strip clubs, whorehouses. I go
where the meetings are. It's my fucking job."*

Your quest for power doesn't clock in at nine and clock out at
five. It doesn't take nights or weekends off. There are no half-
day Fridays, no leisurely mani-pedi lunches at Burke Williams.
It's not home in time to watch Jon Stewart live, and it doesn't
catch the early train out of the city. Your quest for power does
not recognize Columbus Day.

The climb to the top is a 24/7, 365-days-a-year crusade. Once
your work *day* ends, your work *night* begins. What you accomplish between the hours of 7 p.m. and 2 a.m. is just as—if not
more—important than the points you put on the board during
traditional business hours. You can't build an empire isolated in
an office building eight hours a day. Like a politician's daughter
down a well under Buffalo Bill's house—you gotta break free
and get your ass out in the world.

Some of my most legendary work happens outside of the office. More business gets done over cocktails at Sunset Tower and steaks at Craig's than in any sterile boardroom. Dinners, drinks, events, functions—they are all vital to your survival. I've signed clients while motorboating a pair of glittery and desperation-filled double-Ds at the Spearmint Rhino in downtown LA. Closed multimillion-dollar TV syndication deals at 4 a.m. inside an Uber SUV on the way to Vegas. Forged lifelong friendships over a bottle of Château Lafite from the roof of the Hotel du Cap in Cannes at sunrise. Success isn't something that happens inside a cubicle. You have to go where the action is. You have to have as big of a presence outside the office as you do inside of it.

Think of weight lifting. Most regular guys I know who lift only care about their upper body. They want big arms, big shoulders, and a big chest. They often don't work out their legs. But professional bodybuilders know that half of your body mass and testosterone is in your glutes, quads, and hamstrings, and that by working them out, you actually make your upper body that much bigger. The same principle applies to your work life. If you work your ass off all day, only to come home and watch reruns of *Designing Women* on TBS all night, you're not maximizing your gains and achieving your full potential. Working out your legs gets your upper body bigger. The work you do at *night* benefits the work you do during the *day*. One hand serves the other. Don't be the asshole with only one hand clapping. Like a Zamboni clearing the ice—once the sun goes down— it's a fresh rink; time to lace up those big-girl skates and nail some triple fucking salchows à la Michelle Kwan in '98.

My mantra is *Be everywhere.*

Make people think you've been cloned.

One minute you're discussing the hidden opportunities of leaked sex tapes over a martini with Kim Kardashian at the Beverly Hills Hotel, the next you're having dinner with Warren Beatty talking about life before condoms at Soho House.

One day you're pretending like you know who Kelly Ripa's husband is at the White House Correspondents' Dinner in DC, the next you're booking a "de-stress" massage from the Four Seasons in Tokyo before the world premiere of a new *Aquaman* movie.

By attending local, national, and international events you elevate your public profile and increase the chances of serendipitous encounters.

The two most important lessons I can impart here are:

1. Go out every night.
2. Attend as many events as you can (especially ones that would make others jealous if they saw you there on Instagram).

You want people to think of you like a Visa Black Card. You're everywhere they want to be.

Los Angeles is a social town, filled with dreamers, schemers, and in-betweeners. Every night of the week the city's splashy bars and restaurants are filled to the brim with people out carousing, doing business, or some furtive combination of the two. I find many opportunities in life arise by simply putting yourself in the middle of a highly saturated area, then taking advantage of the random and unpredictable collisions that occur inside of it. Bottom line: Go where the action is and bump into people. You'll be amazed at the fortuity that can happen: The interior decorator you meet at a dinner party turns out to be best friends with an A-list actor you're trying to sign; an old college friend you run into at an art gallery in Brentwood gets you into the seed round of Uber; the guy standing in line with you for the pisser at a new SBE club is looking to park a couple hundred million dollars into features. All of these things have happened to me in real life. Of course, it cuts both ways—if you're lucky enough to meet me, your life will be forever changed, probably for the better unless you piss me off or annoy me, and you should get down on your knees and thank whatever god or intergalactic alien ruler you pray to for the privilege and pleasure.

Opportunities are night owls. They like to streak naked and howl at the moon. A lot of success in life comes down to luck. So put yourself in a position to get lucky. Because you know what happens if you don't go out?

Nothing.

When I was an agent, I would try to hit four separate events each evening. I'd usually leave my office at 6:50 p.m. for a 7 p.m. drink; depart the drink by 7:45 p.m. to make an 8 p.m. dinner; I'd dominate the dinner until around 9:30 p.m., at which point I'd bounce out to attend a couple charity events, screenings, music showcases, birthdays, premiere parties, natural childbirthing rituals—whatever relevant functions I needed to make a guest appearance at that night. I tried to spend no more than twenty minutes at each location, a half hour tops. That's more than enough time to be seen by everyone there and to talk to the most important people in the room. This is a pace that doesn't get easier; it actually gets more challenging. The higher up the food chain you climb, the more in demand you'll be. You can send your minions to some events in your stead, but, like a cold bottle of Coca-Cola Classic, you can't beat the real thing. Being social is essential, but make sure business comes at the head of the conversation so you can kick back and be more casual at the tail. Time management is paramount. My internal clock might as well have been made by Breitling, it's so fucking pinpoint. I'm like Good Will Hunting sitting in Mork's office counting the second hand tick by tick. Drinks and dinners and events are usually scheduled weeks in advance, but it's always a fluid situation; something else always pops up last minute and I have to cancel or reschedule. My calendar is like Katy Perry's hair color: Just when you think you know what it is, it changes. Like Muhammad Ali, float like a butterfly and stay light on your feet.

You know how athletes sometimes have to play hurt? Well, sometimes you have to *eat* hurt. Situations will arise where you'll have to attend two, three, sometimes four dinners in the same night. You can't let your companions know this or they'll feel like you're two-timing them with other dinners. So what do you do? You suck in your gut and eat your third goddamn spaghetti bolognese of the night. Like a professional. Like a champion. Then at some point after the meal, excuse yourself to use the restroom, and—like a *Teen Vogue* model the morning before her first big cover shoot—stick your finger down your throat and raise that spaghetti bolognese from the dead. It's not pretty, but you do what you need to do to stay in the game. Successful people do the things that unsuccessful people don't do. Of course, you can always order a hundred-dollar plate of truffle pasta for dinner and not take so much as a bite, which is a bold power move, because at the end of the day, if your primary focus at a dinner is to *eat*, then you're already fucked.

Over the course of any given calendar year there are mainstay events that I will never miss. Below is a breakdown of my Hollywood Social Calendar.

ARI GOLD'S YEARLY EVENT CALENDAR

January. The start of the calendar year. A time for renewed enthusiasm and vitamin-rich IV treatments to combat the inevitable **New Year's Eve** hangover from whatever epic adventure I went on to celebrate. One New Year's Eve, Daniel Day-Lewis and I hiked up to the summit of Machu Picchu and while up there, we co-wrote a sequel to *My Left Foot*, aptly titled *My Right Foot*, which was unfortunately confiscated when the Peruvian military took us into custody and my good friend Bill Clinton had to make a personal phone call to the president of Peru for our release. Another New Year's Scarlett Johansson, Tony Blair, and I secretly brought Skrillex in to spin a black tie party inside the main ballroom at Buckingham Palace; the night is foggy, but I remember a member of the royal family passing out under the DJ booth before midnight after doing too many Whip-its. Another New Year's Eve, I was partying with

Leo and some Victoria's Secret angels at a nightclub in Sydney, Australia—fairly standard; except when the clock struck midnight, we drove to an airfield, jumped onto a private plane, and flew back to California—beating the international time change so we could celebrate the stroke of midnight for a *second* time in Los Angeles at a party inside Adam Levine's newly renovated sex dungeon. I think the same set decorator from *Fifty Shades of Grey* did the décor. If March goes in like a lion and out like a lamb, the end of December goes in like a lion and out like a fire-breathing velociraptor. Some people do New Year's resolutions. Those people are weak. My only resolution is to keep doing what I'm doing. You don't mess with perfection. January is also when I go to the **Sundance Film Festival** in Park City, Utah, a trip comprised of skiing, gifting suites, movie screenings, avoiding Mormons, and partying until sunrise at Tao nightclub (which is essentially just a big tented parking lot with a bunch of floor heaters, but people line up outside swarming to get in like it was Noah's ark and it just started raining). January also marks the beginning of **Awards Season**, with the **Golden Globes** and the **SAG Awards** kicking it off. While the awards shows themselves can be lame, the after-parties are some of the best in town. Last year I accidentally walked in on two award winners penetrating each other with their statues on the rooftop of the hotel. Gold sure can make people do crazy things.

February. The month of February is an awards show whirlwind, starting with the **Grammys**, then the **DGA** and **WGA** awards, followed up by the queen bee of them all, the **Oscars**.

The Grammys are a good time for everyone to get drunk and pretend the music industry is still relevant. By this time next year half of these labels won't exist, and the A/R guys in Armani suits popping thousand-dollar bottles of champagne will be working as interns at Spotify or Pandora. In an ironic twist, I know one former record exec selling fresh oranges in the empty parking lot on Sunset where the Tower Records used to be. Still, music people know how to throw a party, and it's worth attending. And say what you will about the Oscars, but it's still Hollywood's equivalent of coronating royalty. The gold standard of awards shows. The entertainment elite at their finest. People from all over the world watch the aspirational broadcast dreaming someday they too might stand up on that stage at the Kodak Theater and thank the Academy. You've got about as big a chance of that happening as Mickey Rourke does of being named *People*'s "Sexiest Man Alive" these days, but keep dreaming, pal, because *your* dreams fuel *my* business. The one thing you can count on is that I'll be at the ceremony, front table, new tux, every year, until I'm six feet under (and even then I may have them wheel my corpse in for the first posthumous Deathtime Achievement Award). The Oscar after-parties are fine, a bit formal and stuffy for my taste. I think it comes from the feeling of dread many winners face at the realization that their lives will never be any better than they are at that very moment. The **Super Bowl** is also in February, which I go to every year, rooting for whatever team has the most players represented by my former agency (as I still have some skin in that game). I'll usually also hit up the **Berlin Film Festival**, mainly because for the one night I'm there it's fun being the most powerful Jew in Germany, plus I know my ancestors up in heaven are proud every time I take a piss, spelling out G-O-L-D in all caps on the Brandenburg Gate.

March. March is when all the TV pilots my clients booked were shot. The majority of that month was spent traveling from set to set across the country to visit the more successful TV stars, assuaging their fears that their pilot would get picked up, knowing full well that most of them wouldn't and they'd be back to doing guest spots on *Murphy Brown* and *Hangin' with Mr. Cooper* to pay their mortgages. I remember I was a young agent when my client at the time, Scott Bakula, booked the coveted *Quantum Leap* pilot. He was so nervous the show wouldn't go that a patch of his hair turned gray, which only caused him to freak out even more. Turns out that's the defining characteristic that made him famous-ish. In March I'd also attend the **SXSW Film Festival** in Austin, Texas, where I'd usually host a panel on entertainment or give a keynote address about leadership in the workplace, after which I'd take a cheat day and gorge myself on some authentic Texas barbeque from Rudy's, then top the trip off by dropping a freakishly horrendous deuce in the powder room at the governor's mansion, where I always stayed, then "forget" to flush the toilet. In Texas, the size of a man's shit is the size of his worth. They actually believe crap like that down there (no pun intended). So I always like to leave a parting gift poking out the rim from the West Coast.

April. In April I attend the first weekend of the **Coachella Music Festival** out in the Palm Springs desert, usually going with a group of aging technology billionaires and out-of-touch celebrities who hope getting their pictures taken with trendy hipster bands from London's West End will make them feel as young as the high school kids out there on ecstasy going down on one another behind the soundboard. I go because it's a perfect chance to network in the VIP tent while working on my summer base tan. Later in the month is the **White House Correspondents' Dinner** in Washington, DC, which I usually bring Mrs. Ari to; she's an excellent blocker, talking to people beneath me that I don't want to have talk to. This event is an opportunity to connect with some of the biggest media power-houses in the business, several of whom used to be my clients. But the main reason I go, is, of course, to let the president pay me his respects. When I was running Miller/Gold, we always held our **Agency Retreat** in April. This was a company-wide weekend meeting where we would take over a five-star resort, usually in Santa Barbara or San Diego, and review our collective goals for the upcoming fiscal year. And, as if part of some unwritten tradition, every year, an agent would always get an assistant pregnant. Many children today literally owe their lives to two people getting drunk at this retreat and making bad decisions. You're welcome. And although I'm not an agent anymore, I still try to pop my head in every year. Like having a general understanding of the Big Bang theory, it's good for these younger agents to meet and see the man who created their universe.

May. I start off the month of May going to the **Kentucky Derby,** where I usually own a stake in one of the horses running. It's a lot of old people with old money, wearing big hats and pastel suits like they just stepped out of an episode of *Knots Landing*, but despite the humidity, the Confederate flags, and the entire state's turgid hard-on for Colonel Sanders, I get important finance-related business done at this event, and those Kentuckians sure know how to make a mean mint julep. Then it's off to the **TV Upfronts** in New York, a week-long event where TV networks and cable companies hype their new fall programming line-up to advertisers and corporate sponsors to try to sell them commercial ad time on their airwaves. It's big business for the networks, and they go all out to impress their advertising clients. Most people think the lion's share of an agency's revenue comes from its A-list feature film talent, but it doesn't. The primary source of revenue for any successful agency flows from TV packaging and syndication. So while it may look like I was slumming it in TV by going to the Upfronts all those years, I was really servicing the lifeblood of the agency and building a foundation on which my empire could continue to expand. While in New York in May, I also attend the **Met Gala**, an annual fundraising jubilee for the Metropolitan Museum of Art's Costume Institute, but is really just an excuse for celebrities to show off their new plastic surgery in designer formalwear, as well as for Anna Wintour to step outside in daylight hours in her yearly attempt to prove that she isn't a vampire. Toward the end of the month is the **Cannes Film Festival** in the French Riviera. This extravagant celebration of independent worldwide cinema gives me a great excuse to meet new artists from all around the globe, go cliff-diving with Harvey Weinstein, and stay for a couple days on my pal David Geffen's

454-foot yacht out on the Mediterranean. The boat is gorgeous, but it's always a bit of a sausage fest.

June. June is a slower month on the event calendar, which is perfect because by this point in the year I'm ready for a momentary respite in travel to enjoy the replenishing sunshine and warm summer nights in LA. The month of June is why Southern California was invented. June is the heart of summer movie season, so there are plenty of big blockbuster premieres to attend, but most of them are local. The only annual event I attend every year in June is called **E3**. It's the world premier trade show for computer, video, and mobile games. Taking place at the Convention Center in downtown LA, E3 is basically a pregame warm-up to the nerdfest that is Comic-Con, which takes place down in San Diego in July. Nothing fun or interesting ever happens at video game conferences like E3, unless you consider Ice-T letting fans take pictures with his wife Coco's ass on stage while promoting his new *Law and Order: SVU* mobile game fun. One time a developer from Electronic Arts and a developer from Ubisoft got in a fistfight in the middle of the showroom floor, but they both stopped after one punch to take a pull from their respective inhalers and by the time they squared off again security had broken it up.

July. July is always a busy month. My family and I usually spend the **Fourth of July** with Larry Ellison, the founder of Oracle and the third richest man in the world, and his family at his annual billionaire beach blanket bingo bash in Malibu. We used to go to the Hamptons for P. Diddy's White Party, but ever since he played Sidney Poitier's role in the made-for-TV movie version of *A Raisin in the Sun*, no one really goes to that anymore. Then there's **Comic-Con**, which, up until ten years ago, was a small convention where comic book aficionados across America would collectively set their phasers to Nerd and venture west to San Diego to not have sex and celebrate all things cosplay. But ever since film studios' bread started getting buttered by superhero movies—combined with the rising affinity for nerd culture in society because of television shows like *The Big Bang Theory* and everyday techies-turned-billionaires like Mark Zuckerberg and Jack Dorsey—Comic-Con has exploded as the go-to Valhalla for everything geek chic. One time I saw a guy dressed as Uma Thurman's character, Poison Ivy, from *Batman and Robin* and a girl dressed as Uma Thurman's character, Mia Wallace, from *Pulp Fiction* sitting at a table playing Dungeons and Dragons with the real-life Uma Thurman, who was dressed as Lucy Liu's character, O-Ren Ishii, from *Kill Bill*. It was the most fucked-up meta-on-meta thing I'd ever seen. Couldn't help picturing what an Uma-on-Uma-on-Uma three-way would look like and how much I might be able to sell tickets for. Comic-Con is like a bizarro world *Revenge of the Nerds* where the Alphas are outcasts who will never ascend to coolness, and the nerds run the college like the Asgardians in *Thor* rule the universe. Jesus, see, now I'm doing it. Every time I leave Comic-Con I feel like I need to come home and take a bath in Macallan whisky and watch a Steve McQueen movie just to wash the nerd off of me. In August I also attend **the ESPYs** to support all my peeps in the world of sports. Making an appearance and networking at this awards ceremony ensures I never sit anywhere but courtside at a basketball game and have field passes to every Super Bowl. But the most significant and meaningful event I go to every July is the **Allen and Company Sun Valley Conference** in Sun Valley, Idaho—an exclusive gathering of the most powerful media mavens, business leaders, and political figures in the country. From Bill Gates to Larry Page to Warren Buffett to LeBron James to Marc Benioff, the small mountain town in Idaho is overrun each July for one week by the richest one percent in America. Everyone shows up under the guise of attending informational panels and seminars, but really we're all there to get stoned with other rich people, play poker, and find new ways to make money. I get a lot of business accomplished at this conference every year, procuring relevant pieces of information and setting red herrings and misdirects with other titans about my business intentions. It's a bunch of wolves in wolves' clothing at this thing, so you either sharpen your fangs or you'll get slaughtered like a sheep. Same fucking thing.

August. The main event I attend in August every year is the **Venice Film Festival.** I always had a client or two with movies at the fest, but the yearly trip to Italy served a surreptitious dual purpose. From Venice I'd catch a flight to Rome, where I'd meet up with my good friend and fashion designer Valentino Garavani, who would proceed to personally tailor twenty custom suits for me to wear throughout the work year. This is how Ari Gold goes shopping. I'd spend the day with Valentino at his workshop by the Campo de' Fiori, sometimes bringing a special guest along. On one occasion, Vinnie Chase came with me. Valentino fitted us both with some incredible bespoke suits, then we all went to dinner at La Pergola, where Vinnie proceeded to pick up two gorgeous Italian models halfway through the appetizer. By the time we finished dinner we'd had several bottles of wine and it was almost three o'clock in the morning. I was ready to call it and head back to the hotel but Vinnie said, "I know. Let's go check out the Trevi Fountain." Valentino responded, "But it is late. It will be empty. No one will be around." A grin I knew all too well formed across Vinnie's face. "Perfecto." The Trevi Fountain is a popular tourist destination in Rome, made famous by the immortal Fellini film *La Dolce Vita*. There is a security guard posted there twenty-four hours a day to ensure that assholes from other countries don't try to do cannonballs or take a piss in the fountain. When we arrived, the area surrounding the fountain was a ghost town, just a schlubby security guard reading a comic book and eating a Snickers bar at his post. When he looked up and saw Vinnie standing in front of him, I swear this three-hundred-pound tub of SpaghettiOs almost started doing backflips. "Aquaman, you've come to save me!" The guard was so enamored by Vince he gave us carte blanche. Vince was a god, the guard his loyal servant. So Vinnie did the only natural thing anyone who'd played a water-based superhero standing beside the Trevi Fountain at three in the morning with two models could do. He got naked with the girls and went swimming. I have some pictures that will forever remain locked away in my vault of Vinnie, the girls, and the security guard, all standing topless in the middle of the fountain (it's a little off-putting that the security guard's tits are the biggest of the group, but nonetheless, it's a great picture). I think even a man as seasoned as Valentino was impressed. But in Rome magic happens every day. That's why it's Rome. August is also the month when everyone in Hollywood takes their **vacations**. It's similar to spring break in college where everyone in your school goes to one of the same two or three destinations. Hawaii. Saint-Tropez. Cape Cod. Miami. Go to any one of them in August and you're bound to bump into half the people you do business with. I let Mrs. Ari decide where we go. As long as I'm on a beach with a piña colada in my hand, a clear line of sight through my heavily tinted sunglasses to all the young ass parading around the beach practically in dental floss that I can secretly look at but not touch, and the kids are having fun, I'm happy. Toward the end of the month I'd also attend the **Telluride Film Festival** for one night. But being in the woods longer than twenty-four hours, without the city sounds of cars honking, fire engines blaring, and crazy indigents pontificating about the end of the world being nigh, starts to creep me the fuck out.

September. After Labor Day, everyone begrudgingly returns to work with back-to-school blues, having to lube their veins with coffee and Red Bull to clear out the remnants of the summertime hangover and ramp up hard for fall business. Everyone except me, that is, because I'm always ready to go. In September TV heats up as networks bust open their coffers to buy new TV show pitches from writers and showrunners for development season. I used to love intimidating network executives by showing up at pitch meetings unannounced and demanding they buy the show in the room or I would burn the entire building down with them tied up in it. Sometimes life is about the simple pleasures. In September I usually go to **Fashion Week** for a night or two in New York. Why Fashion Week? Because it's populated with A-list actresses who fancy themselves part-time designers because they know how to use Pinterest, and it provides the perfect opportunity to cozy up to them. One rule of business is to go where the other guys aren't. And for the longest time, no other agent ever thought about going to Fashion Week, except for me. It wasn't until a picture of me and Sarah Jessica Parker sitting front row at the Oscar de la Renta show was spread across Page Six that other agents started getting wise to my game and showing up. The downside of having a first-mover advantage is that, eventually, people start to follow you. In September I also attend the **Toronto Film Festival,** which is basically an excuse for Canada to pretend like they're a country of culture and sophistication as opposed to the moose-fucking inbreds who talk like retarded versions of the Minions from *Despicable Me* that we all know they are. Canada's biggest accomplishment is that it's gone its entire existence without actually accomplishing anything, something unheard of for a country of its size. If they gave out a Razzie Award for "Worst Performance Pretending to Be a Real Country," Canada would win it every year. Another big event in September is the Jewish High Holidays, **Rosh Hashanah** and **Yom Kippur.** A time of atonement for Jews, what these holidays really mean is that the town shuts down for a couple days and the handful of Catholics out there get a crack at trying to make something happen.

October. October is a month where everyone seems to be in a festive mood. It's when college and NFL football are back in full swing, the World Series is right around the corner, and the weather gets crisper so everyone can finally start wearing the wool suits and cashmere sweaters they bought on sale at Barneys in April. The **New York Film Festival** is in October, which is a great excuse to visit the Big Apple in the month it was made for. Of course October is also best known for **Halloween**, marking the beginning of the holiday season, which will take us through the end of the year. There are always a handful of epic Halloween parties to attend in the two weeks leading up to the thirty-first. It's important to choose the right ones. Usually a good gauge for Halloween parties or any party in general is that if either Paris Hilton or Pauly Shore are going, you shouldn't be. When it comes to Halloween costumes, I don't wear one. They are beneath me. I always go as myself. When people ask what you're dressed as, tell them, "the future owner of your soul."

November. Nothing happens in November. It's basically a dead month. Similar to the seventh inning stretch of a baseball game, you just want to hurry up and get to the end. Of course, **Thanksgiving** is in November, but that's really just a bullshit holiday put there by our wise forefathers to remind us that Hanukkah and Christmas are right around the corner and it's time to start having your assistant order presents for your wife and kids online before an arctic blast hits and shuts down FedEx's East Coast fleet. Then there's this thing called **Movember**, a pledge some men take to grow out their mustaches for the entire month without shaving, in order to raise money for prostate cancer. First, if you participate in Movember, fuck you. Second, if you want to raise money for prostate cancer (a noble cause), do it the old-fashioned way, by either begging for it or exerting yourself physically for donations. Sitting on your ass and letting nature takes its course above your upper lip is not the same as running a 10K at a local high school or breaking out the set of power tools your dad gave you as a housewarming present collecting dust in your garage and using them to go out and build a habitat for humanity. Maybe I can raise money for rectal cancer by getting people to pledge a dollar every time I take a shit. And third, no one wants to see that horrific seventies pornstache growing like a caterpillar with cerebral palsy zigzagging across your face; you look like you're about to go door to door informing people that you're a registered sex offender who's just moved in next door and would their kids like to come out and wash your windowless van for a dollar? Fuck Movember. And November.

December. The last month of the calendar year is a time for reflection and hurling up Hail Marys like Doug Flutie in 1984. Come the first of December, most people are already mentally checked out on the year, either thinking about their upcoming vacations to Mexico or Hawaii, or about how this Christmas will be the Christmas when they finally come out to their parents. (Come on, you're not fooling anyone. Your parents know your "roommate," Fernando, isn't really a foreign exchange student from Guam.) If you let your telescope fog over in December, you may miss out on treasure ripe for plundering. Most of the time you can squeeze in last-minute deals before the clock strikes midnight. Like the best coaches in the world will tell you—if you want to win, you have to play until the end. For the most part, December is a cavalcade of loud and lustrous holiday parties—one final parade of social events before the fat lady sings. Agency parties. Studio parties. Network parties. Golden Globe nominations. It's a great time to be in Los Angeles; while the rest of the world freezes their asses off in the latest snowpocalypse, we're drinking eggnog and lighting Hanukkah candles on the beach in sandals and board shorts. The last two weeks of December into the first week of January all of Hollywood shuts down like the entire continent of South America during the World Cup. Come to LA during that time and it's a ghost town, like that movie *I Am Legend*. This is when I take my holiday vacation with the family, pulling up a beach as close to the equator as I can get, digging my toes in the sand, and ruminating on the year that was. The reprieve is short but sweet. January lurks right around the corner. Soon the clock starts again. And thankfully so. I can only sit still so long. I get restless if I go more than a week without seeing the inside of a plane. There's too much to do, too much to see, too many places to be in the world to stay grounded. That's just how I'm built. Like Newton said, "An object in motion continues in motion." I shot out of my mom's cooch like a fireball from a dragon's mouth and never stopped moving.

When it comes to attending events throughout the year, don't half-ass anything. Always use your full ass.

NEVER GIVE OUT YOUR NUMBER

Miss Potts was unquestionably the hottest teacher at my private high school. Twenty-nine years old, pencil skirts, librarian glasses, forget about it. I transferred into the school following a string of near-arrests with the "wrong crowd," and Miss Potts immediately took an interest in me. At fifteen, I was five-one and 105 pounds, and my face had not yet grown into my features. I had Hobbit feet and a dirt 'stache, but Miss Potts said I was cute. She spent a lot of time with me after school, frequently offering to drive me home and occasionally giving me "hints" about test and homework answers. I was ready to joust every time she tousled my hair. And she loved to tousle my hair.

I fell hard for Miss Potts, and try as I might to be realistic, I couldn't shake the feeling that my desires were reciprocated. Her long glances, her easy laughter, the fact that she would wait around for me after school day after day... I had to know. My parents were out of town when Miss Potts drove me home one night and I made my move.

"You want to come in for a drink?"

Her look let me know that I had tragically misread the situation. She didn't even respond. She just looked sad and unlocked my door. It was the last ride home she ever gave me. After that awkward moment, I was completely cut off.

That was the last time I ever made the first move—in love, life, or business. Since that horrible evening in my parents' driveway, I have never led with my number at a party or in a negotiation. Like my man Floyd Mayweather, I became a patient counterpuncher, suppressing eagerness and desire on behalf of leverage. I am certain that the strategic advantages of my "you need me more than I need you" attitude have led to millions of dollars of increased revenue for my companies. To that end, one could say that I indirectly owe Miss Potts a ton of cash, and to be honest with you, I would happily toss her a six-figure commission if she agreed to tell me what the fuck she was doing toying with the hormones of a skinny fifteen-year-old kid thirty years ago.

RULE # 9

Pay It Forward So You Get Paid Back

"When you sign with me, what's mine is yours."

Gift giving is one of the most important things I do. Just as every problem creates an opportunity to be a hero, every gift you give is an opportunity to be a star. Make no mistake, it is an art form. And much like the ancient pages of the *Kama Sutra*, it should be rigorously studied, practiced, and mastered.

I'm sure there's an academic study at a university somewhere that proves that the act of opening a gift triggers the same neurons in the pleasure center of the brain as does ejaculating onto a daytime soap star's nose job—but we don't need science to validate this concept. Just look at all the multimillion-dollar tchotchke companies out there making a fortune off rabbit foot key chains and porcelain cat statues. This is why gifting suites exist at film festivals like Cannes and Sundance or any other mainstream event trying to attract celebrities and high-profile people. Regardless of how cultured you are, how rich you are, how famous you are, a free pair of Ugg boots is a free pair of Ugg boots.

Hanukkah was the smartest holiday Jewish toymakers ever invented.

Put simply, people like to get shit.

Real players understand that gift giving is an indispensable weapon in their arsenal for world domination. When architected correctly, the art of the gift separates you from the pack, fashioning a tangible reflection of how you want to be perceived among the world elite.

Nothing makes you look better than giving a thoughtful, spectacular, one-of-a-kind gift to someone you have an important relationship with or someone you're pursuing an important relationship with (aside maybe from having a sex tape released starring you and the latest Guess model...but that's more about self-branding, which we'll review in another chapter).

The reverse is also true.

I've seen business deals shattered, marriages imploded, dynasties crumbled because of careless, ill-conceived gift giving.

Don't believe me?

Next anniversary, come home with some anti-wrinkle cream or a new StairMaster for your wife, then email me and let me know what life is like living at a Red Roof Inn.

If there is one thing and one thing only you take away from this chapter it should be this: When it comes to gift giving, your aim is to give a gift so unique, so specific, so amazingly impossible that the gift itself—along with what you had to do to ascertain it—becomes more than just a *thing* . . . it becomes a *story*.

The masterly gift giver knows that the best gifts exist long beyond the moment they're given. By constructing a narrative around them, they live on into eternity. I call this *Franchising Your Gifts*. Think of it like buying Apple in the seventies. It may be a one-time purchase, but it's going to pay out cash dividends forever.

I sometimes lie awake at night thinking about the perfect gift. It's a precision game. Like rocket science, if you're off by an inch at launch, you'll be off by a mile at landing. One day I'll hire an MIT think tank to sit around all day thinking of gift ideas for me. Let someone else cure cancer, solve climate change, and fix the global population problem. Gifts are important, because gifts help you win.

The good thing is that most people are abominable gift givers.

That's why I love the holiday season so much. When everyone else is giving the same generic bottles of wine, the same canned fruit baskets, the same tired, unexciting bullshit, I'm coming in hot with customized gifts that melt people's faces.

When the president of the United States is having Christmas dinner in the State Dining Room and my gift arrives special delivery during the crème brûlée dessert course, you can be damn sure it's going to be something he'll remember.

When the biggest movie star in the world is vacationing on Steve Ballmer's yacht in the Mediterranean, and my gift arrives at midnight via helicopter, it'll be a story he'll talk about in interviews and on nighttime talk shows forever.

When Hilary Swank look-alike Justin Bieber is neck-deep in Brazilian women somewhere in the favelas of Rio, my surprise gift will be a beacon of light in a time of otherworldly darkness. (By the way, if you really think that little tatted-up rat is worthy of my gift list, maybe you should be reading a book with pictures in it to color instead.)

What exactly do I get them? Each gift is different. Tailored to the individual. Besides, I wouldn't tell you anyway. But—if I do a good enough job, you'll probably hear about it on your own.

The key to masterful gift giving is to be highly in tune with the person you're gifting.

I like to think of every individual as their own kind of fortified bank vault. If you ask the right questions and pay close enough attention, every once in a while the tumblers line up and you can hear the click, at which point you can kick the door open and see what's inside. And if you gain insight into what really lights someone's fire, then you can give a gift that will illuminate their world like a coked-up pinball machine on the Fourth of July, and they will roll out the red carpet for you and give you whatever it is you want.

In this regard, one of the many hats I wear in my life is that of a skillful safecracker.

One time early in my career as a junior agent at TMA, I was doing everything I could to sign a hot up-and-coming actress (I won't mention her name, but let's just say the space thriller she did with Clooney last year wasn't an indie film). I knew she was meeting with other agencies, so I was killing myself looking for an angle. We had a perfectly fine, conventional meeting at my office where we pitched her hard, but probably nothing much different than what she was hearing from everyone else around town. I needed to somehow convey to her that I was different, that I would go the extra mile, that I would kill a Pomeranian for her if necessary.

The opportunity presented itself as I was walking her out.

In the front lobby of the office she made an offhand comment about a painting she liked hanging on the wall. She'd recently moved into a new house and was looking for art.

That's all I needed.

As she was going down the elevator, I raced back to my office and called the valet at the front of the building. I told him to do whatever he had to do, but to make sure to hold her car for ten minutes. In the meantime, my assistant and I sprinted to the lobby, lifted the painting off the wall, flew down the back stairwell, tracked down her new address from a friend, sped over to her house before she got there, and broke in (thankfully her housekeeper was home, but I would not have been above breaking a window).

When she got home five minutes later, the painting was hanging on her living room wall. It had a note attached from me that read, "When you sign with me, what's mine is yours. I'll give you the shirt off my back. Or in this case, the painting off my wall."

By the time I got back to my office she'd called four times, cancelled all her other agency meetings, and signed with me then and there over the phone. It was a triumphant victory.

Every time someone goes over to her house and asks about the painting hanging in her living room she tells them the story. "That's how Ari Gold signed me…" That alone has helped me sign multiple huge clients. It's a gift that keeps on giving.

Remember this—the right gift at the right moment can make the difference between winning and losing.

Think of an exceptional gift as a Trojan horse, and you're the armor-plated soldier hidden inside waiting to pop out and say, "Surprise, motherfuckers!" As the presenter of the gift, your name is forever married to it. The gift's story is also your story. And anytime someone tells your story, you win.

Quick postmortem on the above tale: As I mentioned, I was a junior agent at the time. It wasn't my company yet— meaning, it wasn't my painting. I didn't know whose it was or really anything about art then, for that matter. To me it looked like something anyone with a few cans of primary colors and a vague awareness of shapes could have made. Turns out the artwork was by surrealist Joan Miró, valued at $1.8 million, and on loan to the office from Terrance's (the owner of the agency) private collection. Fuck me. I replaced it with one of those pictures of dogs playing poker. It hung there in the lobby for a few weeks before anyone noticed. The joke was ulti-mately lost on that uptight, bloodsucking bastard, Terrance. Despite getting ripped a second, third, and fourth asshole and subsequently almost losing my job over it, in the end, that $1.8 million painting has paid off in commissions tenfold. All in all a sound investment. Always trust your instinct. That said,

I'll look up the signature on the painting next time before giving it away.

Think of a gift like an iceberg.

At first glance, all you can see is the tip. But beneath the surface lies a hulking mass of ice waiting to be discovered.

A franchisable gift is a metaphorical iceberg—there's more there than initially meets the eye. What do I mean by this?

I once gave Darnell Strom, a big-money screenwriting client of mine at the time who loved smoking cigars, a custom-made cherry wood humidor for his birthday. Knowing my penchant for giving spectacular gifts, he was at first thrown—thinking it a nice humidor, sure, but nothing particularly showstopping, especially coming from me.

That is, until I told him that only two of these humidors existed in the world.

One was made for him. The other for international action star, governor of California, housemaid impregnator, and notorious cigar aficionado Arnold Schwarzenegger.

In fact, I told him I had just gotten off the phone with Arnold, and he couldn't stop raving about how this humidor was the best humidor he'd ever had in his long, illustrious career of premium stogie smoking.

My screenwriting client's attitude transformed instantly. Why?

Because he just crashed into a fucking iceberg, that's why.

Let's analyze what this gift and the context around the gift are communicating like we were deconstructing a Shakespear-ean sonnet from freshman year English.

This gift is saying:

1. I know Arnold Schwarzenegger.
2. Because I know Arnold Schwarzenegger, you know Arnold Schwarzenegger.
3. I got Arnold Schwarzenegger the same gift as you. Therefore, I must value you both equally.
4. Arnold Schwarzenegger loves the gift, thereby validat-ing its worth and prestige factor.
5. You now not only have a humidor, you have one of two *original* humidors, the other owned by Arnold Schwarzenegger.
6. I didn't just give you a box of wood. I gave you a story to tell for the rest of your life, involving Arnold Schwarzenegger.

A great gift has layers.

Now, did I actually get Arnold a matching humidor? Don't be a moron. Of course not! Strom may have com-manded million-dollar paydays from studios that didn't know any better (see the chapter on selling heat), but he was a hack writer. Arnold is a seven-time Mr. Olympia world cham-pion. That lackey wordgrinder wasn't worthy of breathing the same air, much less exhaling the same cigar smoke, as Conan the Barbarian. And if Darnell ever ran into Arnold and told him about the humidor, Arnold would just nod and smile and have security escort him out like he was another deranged fan hoping to be Arnold's sperm donor in the sequel to *Junior*.

To this day I hear Strom still shows off his much-adored "Schwarzenegger humidor" at cocktail parties.

Goes to show, sometimes a cigar box is not just a cigar box.

I read something on a bumper sticker once that has always stuck with me: "People won't remember what you did. People won't remember what you said. But people will always remember the way you made them feel."

Sounds gay, but in my experience I've found that to be mostly true.

In every interaction, I want to make people *feel* something.

I'm a chemical agent. Transforming molecules in the room. I'm either bringing sunshine, lightning, or thunder.

I try to extend that same principle to gift giving.

As such, it's important to note that gifts are not limited to palpable, tangible items.

Just because you can't see it, hold it, or touch it doesn't mean it's not a gift.

In fact, many times the best gifts aren't *things* at all. They're something way more ephemeral. Fleeting. Transitory. And if delivered properly, *magical*. (And not the kind of twisted, S&M, Dungeons and Dragons magic Lloyd and his harem of gay wizard friends play when they come home from work at night, but the type of real-life magic that happens when you deliver the *unexpected*.)

A+ gifts can be presented in the form of a well-told story or a perfectly placed compliment. This variety of gift giving can be just as powerful—if not more so—as a physical object. In such, I make it a strict habit to have five to ten well-rehearsed, blue-chip stories I can tell anytime, anywhere if a conversation becomes stale. These come in handy frequently, especially at dinner parties, social functions, and monotonous business events I have to attend.

"How does a *story* count as a gift?" a feeble, unworthy mind might ask.

Because I'm giving someone something they wouldn't have otherwise had: *An experience.*

When I tell a great story, I give the people the gift of hearing it—of being entertained, captivated, enthralled by it.

In the spirit of great orators like my brother from another mother, the great Martin Luther King Jr.—I fucking move people.

My words change lives, bitch.

Think of it like going to the theater. What you're witnessing is a *performance.* Each line expertly scripted. Every joke perfectly timed. The tension in my voice practiced ad nauseam, yet conveyed with the freshness as if I were vocalizing it for the very first time.

But I'm also providing value beyond mere entertainment. A monkey sticking a banana up his ass is entertaining. A dynamic, well-told story transcends anecdotal amusement. It grants the listener an exclusive level of *access.* Access to information. Access to knowledge. Access to a glamorous and mysterious back room of power and privilege that the bourgeoisie don't get the password to.

My stories contain slivers of juicy gossip or salacious rev-
elations about some of the most famous, celebrated people on
the planet. It's not your fault. You can't help but be intrigued.
Like the great David Copperfield, I'm a seductionist. Except
instead of a wave of the hand, I'm seducing you with a roll of
my tongue.

More than anything, the most powerful gift in telling a
mind-blowing story is the inherent right you give the listener
to *retell* it. Newly armed with a scintillating tale to regale *their*
friends and colleagues with, the audience member becomes the
performer. And in retelling your story, they now become part
of it, spreading your legend faster than chlamydia on Mötley
Crüe's *Dr. Feelgood* tour.

The old maxim "It doesn't matter how they're talking
about you, as long as they're talking about you" couldn't be
more true. A person can retell the story a thousand times, in
their own voice, with their own spin, incorporating their own
flourishes—but I will always be the star of that story. I'm the
source. It's my IP. I just license it to the world for free.

Ultimately, by giving them a shiny yarn to spin, you've not
only increased your brand awareness in circles you may not
have bisected yet, you've made the reteller of your tale look and
feel like a primetime baller in front of his or her peers.

You've helped them spin gold.

This kind of story-based gift giving can boomerang back
in fortuitous ways.

One time I was at a charity benefit in New York when the
guest speaker, an influential senator named Ben Schwerin,
began telling an anecdote about how an unnamed agent in

Hollywood had once managed to surreptitiously import two zebras for his homesick African client into the United States using his connections at the State Department.

It was my story.

Being in politics, the man knew how to command a room and had the audience dying of laughter. When he finished telling the story, I stood up and said, "Senator, I'm Ari Gold. The agent you're talking about. But my client wasn't from Africa; she was from Australia. And it wasn't a pair of zebras; it was a pair of kangaroos."

The senator is now one of my best friends.

Another side benefit to regifted stories is the sweet joy one experiences when enemies hear of your conquests. The look on their faces when someone they're trying to ingratiate themselves with says, "Oh, you're an agent? You know, I heard the most amazing story about an agent the other day. Do you know Ari Gold?"

Drives them crazy. The ultimate fuck-you. Sweeter than that first soul-crushing blowjob an aspiring actress from Kansas gives to get a commercial audition upon arriving in LA. It's similar to having a client win an Oscar and being the first person they thank in their awards speech. You're sitting in the theater, not watching the client, but staring down your competition across the room, grinning as they eat a twelve-inch shit sandwich at the table of your immaculate glory. Eat up, cocksuckers.

The bottom line is that you should perfect some awesome stories and gift them like strategically placed land mines. When they detonate, they explode everywhere and no one knows what the hell hit them.

Another important rule is that you should never brag about the gifts you give. If they're remarkable enough, other people will brag about them for you.

I was at a group dinner with a movie star client one time and he was shitfaced and rambling on about how after one of his films hit $300 million in worldwide box office he gave each one of his best friends, friends who'd been with him since the beginning of his career, a million dollars in cash in a briefcase.

A million dollars. In cash. In a briefcase.

Everyone at the dinner was kissing his ass and stroking his ego, telling him how selfless and magnanimous he was, the way people do around self-involved celebrities.

At one point he looked over to me, all boozy and glassy-eyed, and asked, "Ari, what do you think? You ever heard of anyone doing something like that?" I looked him straight in the face and said, "It's a generous gesture. No argument there. But that story is only okay if *someone else* is telling it. Coming out of your own mouth, you sound like a narcissistic asshole."

Sure, he fired me right then and there. But I was right. And I'd rather be right and suffer for it than obsequious and benefit. (Of course, he rehired me a week later because I'm the best, apologizing for overreacting. Actors.)

When someone else brags about a gift you gave, it's complimentary and effective. When you do it, it's classless and tacky.

When you are the recipient of a gift, accept and use it graciously. How you respond to a gift can become a return gift in and of itself. Wear the watch you were given to courtside seats at the Lakers game and make sure to flash it to the cameras. Put the borderline inappropriate Nubian fertility statue from your friend's safari to Africa in the entryway of your home when he comes over (then promptly remove it after he leaves). Bring the bottle of wine you received as a thank-you gift to a group dinner and tell everyone there *who* gave it to you, knowing it will get back to that person. Most of this should be common sense, but there are a lot of dipshits out there, so I figured I'd write it down in case you're one of those special-needs kids who need more hand-holding.

So, what's the end result of all this strategy and elbow grease and deep thinking when it comes to gift giving? The ability to give someone something special and singular can ingratiate you into their lives forever. If you can give a gift that isn't just a *thing*, but a prized possession—an artifact—that becomes part of someone's story, part of their *narrative*, then you have won.

Ultimately this approach may be more challenging and time-consuming in the short term, but the cost/benefit ratio of giving bespoke gifts pays out exponentially in your favor in the long run. If there is one thing we've learned so far it's that short plays have their place as you move up the mountainside—but it's the long con that gets you to the summit in the end.

It's like a karmic mutual fund. The more you put into it, the more you'll get out of it. You won't ever know precisely how the return will manifest, just that it will. No one knows how this stuff works. It's one of life's great mysteries. Like Donald Trump's hairpiece. These things function beyond the realm of human comprehension.

I'm no gypsy hipster mystic; I don't believe in astrology or chakras or any of that late-night Dionne Warwick infomercial, tea leaf, unleash your inner child, find your identity in a tarot card of some faceless bitch holding a ruby scepter and pointing to the sunrise bullshit. (Although I did visit a fortune-teller once in college, way before Mrs. Ari came into the picture. The fortune-teller predicted I was about to release some long-percolating internal tension. As I was bending her over her crystal ball a few minutes later, I realized, wow, she was right! Maybe there is something to this?) But there are invisible forces at work in the universe, and if you know how to make them work for you (or at least not piss them off), life will feel like you're wearing Gollum's Precious on your pointer finger while simultaneously finger-blasting Cleopatra's butthole with your pinky. Ultimate power.

RULE #10

Keep a Scorecard for Favors

"Ease up, man. It's my frickin' party here."

I have done more favors for Hollywood careers than Botox. Everyone in Los Angeles owes me, from the biggest stars to the guys who park cars. Brad Pitt never would have been voted "Sexiest Man Alive" if I hadn't introduced him to kettlebells and marrow cleanses. Emma Stone would still be doing Mattress Depot commercials if I hadn't passed her headshots along to Judd Apatow. Don't get me started on Taylor Swift. Over the past twenty-five years, I've been responsible for more hookups than Tinder and facilitated more connections than LinkedIn and Verizon combined. When it comes to big entertainment deals and careers, I'm like Kevin Bacon, baby—everything and everyone can be traced back to me.

And I keep tabs.

Seventeen years ago, one of my clients was up for a role in *Pearl*

Harbor, which was being directed by Michael Bay. When I heard *Harbor* was green-lit, I sent Michael a bottle of Johnnie Walker Blue along with a note reminding him about my client. Two hours later, the bottle was back in my office, unopened, with a note that said "I don't take bribes." *What?* I was shocked, stunned, and honestly a little hurt. Had Michael Bay forgotten how down he was when I rescued him from the set of a video for something off of Meat Loaf's *Bat Out of Hell II* and magically transported his manscaped ass to a luxury trailer on a credible studio production?

I was appalled by the disrespect, but I also realized that I had no proof of the favor I had done for Bay back in the day. No dates, no records, nothing. It was just Michael Bay's word against mine. Obviously, my word was (and is) worth a lot more in Hollywood, but the experience got me thinking about how ridiculous it was that I didn't have a file for favors. Why wasn't I tracking my social capital? I opened up a new spreadsheet right after I called one of the *Pearl Harbor* producers and convinced him that Kate Beckinsale could act.

Over the years, the little spreadsheet I created in the wake of the Michael Bay fiasco evolved into a full-on Favor Matrix. I even brought in a former Cisco engineer to knock off Quick-Books and then cross-breed the code with industry-leading CRM software in order to provide the perfect mix of relationship management and personal accounting. Not only do I track "transactions"—i.e., the act of doing the favor—but I also track the value of each gesture over time. When I introduced Seal to Heidi Klum, the social debt was significant. When I introduced Brian Austin Green to Megan Fox...well, I'm probably not calling in that marker anytime soon.

Here are my basic rules for maximizing the value of your favor portfolio:

Stay in the Black. Always pay back favors quickly and with a more valuable favor than you initially received. Also, accompany your gesture with a handwritten thank-you note. Notes are genuinely meaningful and, more importantly, also serve as a written record that you have made good on your debt so Billy Baldwin won't keep hitting you up for Lakers tickets two decades after he got you into the *Sliver* premiere after-party. Motherfucker owed me a favor for abandoning me with Tom Berenger.

Obligation is exposure. When you owe someone a favor, a cloud of anticipation will move in and hover over your desk, waiting for the most inopportune moment to shower disruption into your life. The interest on a ride to the airport greatly exceeds a one-time cab charge. Furthermore, you have to train your people in the art of the favor markets so that they don't elevate your exposure without you knowing it. For years, my wife was my biggest favor liability. She would ask her friends for worthless favors, like saving seats for us at a Jewish Community Center production of *Hello, Dolly!* and then two weeks later I would start getting emails with screenplays attached.

Always run a surplus. Think of yourself like a nation. Not America, but a more responsible trading partner, like Norway or Canada. When you export more favors than your trading partners, you gain diplomatic leverage.

Dodge Fractional Repayment. In the winter of 2007, I received a call in the middle of the night from a senior production company executive with whom I was producing a film. Her eighteen-year-old son had been arrested for selling weed at Harvard-Westlake, a prestigious private high school in the Valley, and was facing expulsion and potentially jail time. Worse, the weed he was selling came out of his mother's stash. I woke my wife up laughing.

I made a few calls to friends in law enforcement and the school and managed to make the drug problems go away before other students and parents at the school got wind of what had been going on. Now, it goes without saying that this was a life-changing blue-chip favor, and the producer owed me big-time. I knew it, she knew it, and she smartly wanted to get out of my debt as soon as possible. Problem for her was I didn't need anything. I saw her on the set of our film a few days later and she couldn't look me in the eye. That night, the offers started pouring in. She called and asked if my wife and I wanted to borrow her cabin in Tahoe. I told her I appreciated the offer, but work was crazy and I didn't think we'd be able to take the time away. The following week she called again. Somehow she had found out that my niece was on the waiting list at Berkeley and she offered to grease the admissions department. Again, a nice gesture, but I wasn't about to let her pay me back indirectly. Besides, I already had a handshake deal for my niece at Stanford.

Desperate for closure, the producer eventually offered to suck my dick like the crack fiend in *Menace II Society*.

For a favor the magnitude of saving her son's future, I was not about to accept any repayment below market value. On the Favor Matrix, I categorize life-altering favors as lifelines. Lifelines are get-out-of-jail-free cards for my family and myself. They help me sleep soundly at night, and I would never compromise a good night's sleep for a weekend in Tahoe or a middle-aged hummer.

Learn to Indirectly Communicate Obligation. My favorite feature of the customized Favor Matrix is the auto-alerts feature that connects to my email. Whenever I correspond with a contact who owes me a favor, I receive a color-coded alert corresponding with the gravity of their debt, kind of like America's terrorist threat levels. The alerts allow me to tactfully and indirectly remind the contacts in question of said debts.

"Sounds like a great project. Keep my girl in mind for the guidance counselor role. Say hi to Melinda [who now has a rocking body because I helped her jump a six-month waitlist at the best plastic surgeon in Beverly Hills] for me and have a great week!"

Sending holiday cards, sharing a video, or simply saying "Happy birthday" on Facebook will all refresh favor debt awareness. Again, you're not trying to collect on the debt. You just want to trade on the credit for as long as possible, like Jon Heder with *Napoleon Dynamite*.

Repo Unpaid Favors. There is no statute of limitations on favor repayment. When I am forced to call in an old obligation (doesn't happen often) it's generally more of a repo operation in which I reclaim the social equity without notification and then inform the affected party at a later time. The repo situations tend to be moments in which I need to take action quickly and decisively, like when one of my former assistants, Josh Weinstein, tried to poach Vincent Chase in 2006.

Weinstein met Vinnie initially while discussing a movie,

Clouds, which had been written by his client, Billy Walsh. Weinstein was a brand new agent at the time, and, as newly promoted agents are prone to do, he was living the dream. After years in the mailroom and (later) answering phones for other agents, the cash and cachet that comes with being promoted can be intoxicating. I blew ten grand in Vegas, got four speeding tickets, and had a threesome with the mayor's aide and a Laker girl my first *week* after being promoted. Anyhow, Weinstein was still riding that high and he had yet to test the limitations of his newfound pull when he ran into Vince and his boys at a celebrity art show and immediately invited the whole gang to his house in Malibu for an all-day beach party. His real goal was to show Vince a good time, talk some shit about me, and then convince my client to jump ship. Unfortunately for Josh, I was tight with his boss, Ben Epstein, the actual proprietor of the house Josh claimed to own in Malibu.

I caught Weinstein totally off guard when I burst into the bungalow, which was packed with beer-ponging bros and eager bikinis. Josh puffed out his chest and tried to play man of the house.

"Hey, Ari. You crashing parties now?"

He was holding court with several aspiring *Wild On!* hosts. I addressed them. "Y'know Joshy here—I don't know if you guys know—he used to be my assistant."

"That was a long time ago, Ari."

"Fourteen months. That ain't that long." I put my arm around him like I was his daddy, and smiled at his friends. "He used to make the best hazelnut latte. He was like a chemist in there, working. Just like mommy made."

"Ease up, man. It's my frickin' party here."

"Does your boss know that you're using his house? 'Cause I put a call in to him."

The color drained from Josh's face as I continued.

"Yeah, we went to school together. I helped him cheat on his economics final. That's how he got his degree. He owes me big-time."

I went on to assure Josh that, although I didn't normally steal clients, his whole book of business was about to get got. His B-level sitcom stars, reality TV writers, all of them were in play. I'm pretty sure the kid started crying after I dropped the mic and left with my clients.

I never actually called Weinstein's boss. The repo favor, in this case, was that I invoked Epstein's name in Epstein's house in order to belittle one of Epstein's employees. Not nearly as big a deal as helping Epstein himself graduate from college, but knowing that I could play king of another man's castle without any repercussions gave me the platform to protect my client relationship and squash my immature young enemy.

It was a worthwhile repo.

RULE #11

When I Look in the Mirror, I See a Better-Looking George Clooney

"In the fifteen minutes I have a day free, I take time to keep this body fit, and not just so you have a great ass to look at. I want to live."

A person decides if they want to have sex with you within the first fifteen seconds of meeting you. This is a scientifically proven fact. Over centuries of evolution our eyes and visual cortexes have become so acutely trained to gauge infinitesimal measurements of symmetry and attractiveness in others that before you even have a chance to say, "'Sup, girl?" your fate— one way or the other—is pretty much already sealed. (Beer goggles notwithstanding.) Despite what your varicose-veined Aunt Brenda will tell you, looks absolutely matter. First impressions are always based on appearances. You know within the first fifteen seconds of meeting a blind date if you're doing a table for two at Mastro's or a darkened back booth at Barney's Beanery. You don't swipe right on Tinder because someone looks like they have a good personality. You may argue that this is a shallow way to see things, but that doesn't change the fact that it's true. Humans are visual creatures. It's how our brains are hardwired. Optics are the first line of defense, and books are *always* judged by their covers. It's not until after we've passed through the first checkpoint of aesthetically qualifying someone that we consider other designating characteristics such as intellect, social standing, bank account, and does she summer in Westhampton or Amagansett? Those first fifteen seconds can make you or break you, so why wouldn't you want to look your best? Like the guy on the Head and Shoulders commercial says, "You only have one chance to make a first impression." Yet, every day men and women walk this planet like they just left a fashion seminar taught by the Unabomber. They unfurl their fat rolls at the beach like they're attending a Pillsbury Doughboy convention. They show up to work in oversized khakis with the same twelve-dollar Supercuts hatchet jobs they've sported since repeating the first grade. Your appearance is the story you tell the world. What do you want that narrative to be? I'm an out-of-shape fuckhead and don't give a shit about myself, so why should you? Or, I'm a put-together, confident baller—someone whose genitals you'd enjoy drinking a bottle of rosé off of?

When I look in the mirror, I see a better-looking George Clooney.

Do you?

Here's some thoughts on how you find your inner Cloon:

Accept that we live in an image-conscious world. This isn't up for debate. No one understands this better than my close personal friend Richard Branson. The hip, renegade CEO of the Virgin Group, he looks and dresses like he's an international rock star about to embark on a world headlining tour. Branson knows that the image he projects is psychologically associated with his company. Virgin is cool because Richard Branson is cool. When we had dinner a few weeks ago he told me that he's actually wanted to cut his hair since the early eighties, but he has to keep it long for business.

See first impressions as first opportunities to win. Think of a first impression as your first chance at getting what you want. It's the equivalent of starting the game by passing Go and collecting two hundred dollars versus being stuck in jail and having to bribe your way out. Your appearance is the candy-coated shell that helps the medicine you're selling go down sweetly. One of my buddies from middle school, Todd Waldman, is now the most successful used car salesman in all of Houston, Texas. Why? Unlike everyone else at his dealership, he wears custom tailored suits to work. Who would you rather buy a used Honda from, the guy wearing a stained polo shirt or the guy wearing a designer Zegna suit? He closes the majority of his sales on first impressions. I started out in the mailroom. I was a nobody. But I dressed and acted like I owned the fucking agency. So when I'd go to a club or a dinner and say I worked at TMA, ropes opened. They didn't know I was sorting mail and sucking shit all day.

Be fuckable. Some people come out of the womb looking like an Abercrombie model, others like a descendent from the bloodline of Quasimodo. All you've got to work with is what your momma gave you. Regardless of your physical qualities or lack thereof, your goal is to uncover the best version of yourself and put it on display in a storefront window for the world to judge.

You may still be ugly as fuck, but on the ugly scale spectrum, you're the *hottest* version of ugly. Degrees matter. And while you want to be as fuckable as possible, another way to phrase this would be: Don't be *un*fuckable. When asked about yourself as a sexual entity, you don't want to hear feedback like "Ugh, I wouldn't fuck that guy in a million human or dog years," or "I wouldn't fuck that guy if he had the last human penis on Earth," or "I'd rather chop my hand off and use my bloody stump to pleasure myself than let that guy's naked flesh come within one hundred yards of my fallopian tubes" coming back at you. You need to get your physique, at the barest of bare minimums, to the point where another human being wouldn't want to stab themselves to death with a butter knife at the idea of copulating with you. Think of yourself as a Mr. Potato Head. Mr. Potato Head has a lot of different parts and pieces and ways to arrange himself. Put yourself together so you're the kind of Mr. Potato Head that people want to fuck.

When you look good, you feel good. When I walk into a room, you can feel my confidence radiating like plutonium-239 isotopes at Fukushima. It's because I know I look good. There's a direct correlation between how you perceive yourself and the level of confidence you project. Do you think I enjoy waking up at 5 a.m. to run three miles in the dark every morning? No, I'd much prefer to lie in bed and try to slip it to my wife and pretend I'm sleepwalking. But I run because it makes me look good, which in turn makes me feel good. It's how on any given Sunday, with the right combination of alcohol and stick-to-it-ness, a five can take down an eight. You blitzkrieg someone with lightning confidence and their defenses will fold faster than the Germans at Stalingrad.

So, maybe you're sitting there on your generations-old couch in your parents' basement, drinking your sixth Diet Dr Pepper of the day, wearing unwashed pajama pants and a "Who Farted?" T-shirt, wondering if Kevin Smith is actually a warlock or a male witch, and what exactly are the differences between the two, when all of a sudden you get a glimpse of a pop-up ad featuring a half-naked *Sports Illustrated* model on the Candy Crush game you're playing, and think to yourself, *What can I do to be more fuckable?* Well, here are a few general categories to improve your odds:

Physique. Bottom line, you want to look good naked. With the lights on. You don't have to be shredded like you're about to fight alongside Gerard Butler at the Battle of Thermopylae, but you shouldn't look like you're going as Jabba the Hut's stunt double for Halloween, either. Join a gym. Run. Sweat to the oldies with Richard Simmons. Get lap-band surgery Randy Jackson–style. It doesn't matter. When I used to represent super-buff cage fighter turned actor Jordan Brown, he would always try to find a way to take his shirt off in a meeting for just this reason. Maybe a director didn't think he had the acting chops to carry the part. Or the producers didn't think they could get the movie financed behind him. Or the leading lady wouldn't read with him until he took a shower. Whatever the reason, he'd always find some way to take his damn shirt off, in turn blinding the room with his sculpted physique. It was a great distraction technique, usually swaying things his way. "So what if he can't read. The man looks good naked." Bottom line, get in shape. People have been telling you this since you faked a spinal cord injury in high school so you wouldn't have to expose your fat ass in the group showers after gym class. Girdles are not permanent solutions. Vertical stripes aren't that slimming. Get healthy. You and your diabetes-free body will thank me later.

When it comes to plastic surgery, some people are anti, but I say if it makes you feel better about yourself without turning you into the Cat Lady or the woman from *Cougar Town* who used to be Courteney Cox, then why not? I've seen a doctor's scalpel literally turn a frown upside down. Careers have been extended way beyond their sell-by date from a nip here and a tuck there. Just be cautious. For every Jennifer Aniston, there's a Jennifer Grey. (Turns out a bad nose job will put Baby in the corner.) When used fastidiously and in moderation, creams, gels, injectables—all that crap—can help turn back the clock. It isn't the fountain of youth, but it can lend you some Benjamin Button sorcery for a time, at least until stem cell technology arrives to transform us all back into our sweet-sixteen selves.

Everybody hears the footsteps. You can only hope that when they come for you you've got an extra $50K lying around and a tight-lipped doctor in Beverly Hills on standby to rejuvenate your melting face.

Clothing. One of the best pieces of advice I ever got was from this old mobster named Johnny Abrams, affectionately known throughout the neighborhood as "the Kid," who lived down the street from me growing up. When I knew him he was run-down and could barely walk, so when I'd pass by his house I'd walk his newspaper in the drive up to him on the porch and shoot the breeze for a couple minutes. Of all the sketchy players on my block, he was always kind to me, giving me a quarter or a piece of candy whenever he'd see me on the street. I'll never forget one time he said to me, "Kid, the three most important relationships in your life are with your maker, your mother, and your tailor. And of the three, your tailor is the most important." Now, I've never seen an episode of *Project Runway*, and I fell asleep halfway through the premiere of *The Devil Wears Prada*, but I've been around long enough to know that your clothes shouldn't hang off your body like you're about to go wingsuit jumping off Meru Peak in India. Yet, you see guys walking around today wearing clothes that look more like car covers for their VW buses than apparel. When I was an agent I wore power suits every day, not only as a sign of respect to the talent I represented and the serious work I was there to do on their behalf, but also because it was armor. I strapped it on every morning and went to battle. I felt invincible. To achieve this effect, you need a good tailor. If you don't feel like James Dean in his red leather jacket every time you put a piece of clothing on, then you're doing it wrong.

Grooming. Unless you're in an early seventies–era Eagles cover band, a founding member of a religious cult, or sleeping under a bridge in Seattle, lose the beard and get a haircut. Power doesn't have time for any form of hirsute hipster self-expression.

When I first started out in the mailroom, I decided that in order to combat looking as young as I did, I would grow a beard. After about three weeks, it was starting to come in pretty nicely when my boss at the time, a conservative straight shooter named Jarrad Paul, now a gubernatorial candidate in California, came into the office and said he needed to speak with me, alone, in the conference room. Curious, I walked into the conference room to find five senior assistants and agent trainees all waiting for me, one of them holding an electric razor. Before I knew what was happening, they lifted me onto the table, held me down like they were performing surgery without any anesthetic, and shaved my beard off. When they were finished, I lay there, traumatized, three weeks of hard-earned facial hair growth all around me. Jarrad stood over me and said, "Gold, we'd rather you look young than look like a rapist. From here on out, keep it smooth." I took that lesson to heart, and haven't had more than two or three days of stubble since.

There's a reason cavemen started to develop sophisticated tools before the meteor wiped them all out: It's so they could fucking shave. Do you know how frustrating it must have been to be hunched over all night trying to start a fire only to finally succeed just to have your beard go up in flames? No aloe vera back then. Also, when it comes to grooming, daily showers, deodorant, and general personal hygiene aren't optional. This isn't a sit-in with Joan Baez at Berkeley. Styles may change, but smelling like a hospital room full of geriatric men on dialysis just gave you a golden shower is never fashionable.

At the end of the day, you want to look the best you can. So, be like me and start your morning with a couple handsome sandwiches for breakfast. It's the most important meal of the day.

■ GOLD NUGGET ■
JERK BEFORE WORK

This town is tough. Everywhere you look there are gorgeous bodies you will want to fuck, and beautiful faces you will think about while you are having sex with your spouse. So make sure you rub one out before you get to work, or at least have sex early in the morning. This is one hundred percent imperative, because you do not want to be in the office horny when *Sports Illustrated* swimsuit models show up desperate for jobs or looking to be signed.

RULE #12

When They Say It's Not Personal, Take It Very Personally

"Sticks and stones. Don't throw away a movie just because you can't get along."

In life and in business, it's always personal. Always. When you get let go due to "corporate downsizing," or a studio decides to go another way on a project due to "creative differences," or someone you're dating abruptly cuts it off because "you always have to go to a 'meeting' right after you come on my back"— trust me, it's personal. It may be a business-based decision, but despite what people will lead you to believe, all business is personal.

The key is acting like it isn't.

Easier said than done. Behaving like a personal attack *isn't* personal feels contradictory and counterintuitive; your instinct will be to fan the flame of emotion and blindly retaliate with everything you've got. But there is a fine line between knowing you want to launch a nuclear assault on someone who has wronged you and actually pressing the button. That fine line is what separates the masters from the masturbators, the great divide between wearing the crown on the throne and admiring the way it sparkles from the nosebleeds.

A few years back I packaged a huge summer blockbuster for one of the major studios in town, which means that I brought both the writer-director and the star of the film to the project. The studio originally had a different actor attached to the project, but I convinced his agent that the lead role was too gay for his client, who had just come off a movie involving two dudes, a mountain, and a lot of anal penetration. Being the lazy bastard that he was, the other agent never read the book upon which the film would be based. He just knew that his client would be spending a lot of time on a mountain, alone with another dude, and he panicked. His guy dropped out and my guy, Vincent Chase, stepped in.

Unfortunately, and somewhat ironically, my psychotic insecure writer-director client, Billy Walsh, also became convinced (by the strung-out slam piece he was living with at the time) that the storyline of the source material was, in fact, too gay, so he decided to dump the book that the studio had already paid him half a million dollars to adapt. Instead, my boy, Billy, queefed out one hundred and fifty pages about non-unionized farmhands who battle aliens during the apocalypse. Worse, Billy sent the script to the studio without telling me about it, which meant that instead of coasting to the easy seven-figure payday I worked so hard to set up, I was instead faced with a career-stunting conflagration for two of my clients, not to mention that one of the studio executives, Dana Gordon, was threatening to hold me personally responsible for said blaze, insulting me personally at every turn. I had to stick my fist in my mouth to keep from verbally lashing back at her, but I knew keeping this deal together was more important. For now.

Luckily, I found out about Walsh's change of heart before the chairman of the studio at the time, Richard Wimmer, which meant I still had a few hours to come up with a solution to save Gotham. The first thing I had to do was find out how deep the well was, so I went out to find Walsh. He lived in a pretentious bungalow in one of those LA neighborhoods where lazy hipsters drink vegan lattes and talk about how they're making society better by adopting pit bulls and shopping at consignment stores. Keep in mind, every hour I'm away from the office costs me money, and I almost never drive east of La Brea, but in this case there was too much on the line to troubleshoot remotely.

I walked into Walsh's house and asked him if he was prepared to give back the $500K the studio paid him to adapt the book and, predictably, he told me the money had been spent and he had no intention to ever write the script the studio wanted. When I informed him that the studio would be well within their rights to incinerate his million-dollar hipster hovel with a legal fireball, he unleashed a barrage of personal insults and epithets, attacking everything from the cut of my suit to my worth as a human being, ultimately proclaiming, "You are no longer my agent!" Moments later Dana Gordon called, screaming into the phone, "If I have to tell Richard Wimmer that we lost a script, a director, and a star today, all of whom are your fucking clients, you can bet your ass that nobody who has ever been close enough to smell your breath will ever be welcome at this studio again."

Around lunch, Vinnie dropped the second bomb of the day: He loved Walsh's script and, in typical spoiled movie star fashion, pledged to walk off the project unless Walsh was part of the deal.

When Vinnie told me he was going to walk off the *Clouds* project, I started brainstorming ways to kill Walsh off the project and make it look like a suicide. Then it hit me: Sometimes the best way to solve a problem quickly is to convince people that there is no problem at all. I pulled a U-turn in the middle of Santa Monica Boulevard and gunned it over to the studio, calling Dana on the way and telling her that her best move was to make *Silo*, the script that Walsh had turned in. Her response was, "After this town hears how you tried to bait and switch this studio, it will be your ass that needs saving, you motherfucking piece of shit cocksucker!" I ignored all of it, water off a duck's back. Focus.

At the studio I burst into Richard Wimmer's office right as he was stepping out of the bathroom. Before the guy could get a word out, I told him that *Clouds* had died but I was there to save the day. At this point, Wimmer called Dana into his office and asked what the hell was going on, informing me, "You and your friend Billy Walsh are fucking dead, Ari. You piece of shit!"

It was my show, and like the Reverend Martin Luther King Jr., I started selling the dream of Walsh's farming/fighting script, which, of course, I had not read. At one point I turned to Dana Gordon and asked her, all personal bullshit aside, what she thought about the script, which I knew she hadn't read, either. Dana had to decide: Did she want to oversee a "go" movie or get a job at Telenova producing live Ricky Martin concerts? When Dana told Wimmer that the film was basically *Blade Runner* meets *Field of Dreams*, he green-lit the project in the room, then said, "You made this good, Dana. And you, Ari, this I won't soon forget."

Because I took nothing personally (while knowing all of it was very personal) and forged ahead, I once again turned water into wine.

It's okay to *take* something personally, and, in fact, you should—cataloging and storing it in your memory banks for reference later when an opportune moment arises to enact your revenge upon your enemy—but you should not *appear* to take it personally.

Be a robot. *You* are the droid you're looking for. There's a reason our government has poured years of time and resources into developing AI and robotics warfare studies. Robots are emotionless. Objective. Dispassionate. Void of making mistakes based on pride or sentimentality. All about moves and countermoves. Robots don't get rattled. And neither must you. Clinical in your cunning and demeanor, you can't let emotions get the best of you; they're often less a tuning fork and more a seductive buffet of red herrings, vying to lead you down a calamitous path. I may have a famous temper, but there is always logic behind my outbursts, a method to my emotional terrorism.

When you react to something personally, you become more susceptible to making mistakes. Oftentimes an enemy is goading you with this notion in mind, hoping you'll fall into an artfully constructed trap. Sometimes you need to unleash wrath in response like the ten plagues of Egypt, raining hellfire and damnation, but you need to be savvy enough to know when to give in to emotion and when to table it in exchange for logic and reasoning. I can't teach you that lesson. All I can say is that scorched earth is a strategy you want to use sparingly. Avoid wrestling with a pig; you'll get covered in mud and the pig will end up enjoying it.

On the flip side, if you can incite an emotional response from an adversary, you can create wildly promising opportunities. If you can provoke an enemy to misstep and react heatedly, they become vulnerable and you can use it to your advantage.

I have a therapeutic outlet that hangs from the ceiling of my home gym. It's a custom-made heavy bag, designed with a plastic sleeve at the top that allows me to put a picture of someone's face inside of it. I can release all my physical and emotional aggression onto the bag, punching, elbowing, roundhouse kicking that person's face—exorcising the emotional rage demon in the comfort of my own home without bringing any ruinous emotional detritus into the real-world business octagon. Dana Gordon. Billy Walsh. Richard Wimmer. All faces that have graced my punching bag a time or two. Sometimes I'll go back through the stack of headshots I've metaphorically TKOed over the years and laugh. You'd be amazed how many of them suffered less than stellar professional fates. I'm not saying there's any juju in it, but if you look at the test results, having your face on my punching bag is bad for your health.

From the beginning of time until the end of time people will talk shit. Cavemen were doing it when dinosaurs roamed Earth. I'm sure we'll still be doing it when whatever intelligent alien life out there invades and enslaves our planet. Shit talking is human nature. But it's all noise. Sticks and stones. Some of my best business deals have been done with people who, not a month before, were lambasting and excoriating me all over town to anyone who would listen. Put it in the vault for later use, sidestep it, and look at the opportunity at hand.

Don't ever let emotions get in the way of good business.

Take everything personally; just don't show that you do.

The following is a series of emails between one-time wunder-kind writer Bill Bickley and me when I was his agent. Bickley created the ABC hits *Family Matters* and *Step by Step*, which ran respectively from 1989 to 1998 and 1991 to 1998 and sold into syndication, earning Bickley in excess of $200 million. Below he's getting butt hurt over a critic's review of his new-est pilot, *Just Sayin'*. At the moment, Bickley lives in Nassau County, where he has been working on his biography, which he plans to self-publish. This was our exchange:

Dear Ari—

I must say it's been a while since we've interacted like in the good old days. First off, let me congratulate you on your incredible success. While I won't be so bold as to say as one of your first clients I jump-started your career, you will forever be my agent (even if I can only get your assistant on the phone now, ha ha). Anyway, I have a small problem, and I would be honored if your greatness would take a stab at solving it. This Variety *reporter, Brian Lowry, has set his sights at ruining my latest show,* Just Sayin', *calling it "an insulting, elitist romp through Middle America." If you read the pilot, you would know that there are both Latinos and Asians in the apartment building (residents, not just workers). Lowry's simply an ass with a computer and a power trip. Anything we can do?*

—Bill

Bill—

    Live well, Bill, it's the greatest revenge.

—Gold

Hey Ari—

    I don't mean to be pushy, and I know you are a very busy guy, but this is important, and I really don't ask much of you. As I stated rather generously in my previous email, you are still my agent. Perhaps you're pissed that I haven't been in touch and then sprung this on you. I would love to get dinner. Perhaps the Grill (on you, ha ha). Just please do something about this guy first.

—Bill

Hey Bill—

Any suggestions on what you'd like me to do? Would you like me to have him killed?

—Gold

Ari—

I'd like you to at least get angry. Show some emotions. Like I used to show sympathy for you back in the '90s, when I was flush full of cash and you were just a lowly assistant getting blown off by strippers at Crazy Girls.

—Bill

Bill—

I am angry, Bill. So angry that you, a man who made 200 million green American dollars, can spend time worrying about what Brian Lowry thinks. So take comfort in that and go sit by your Olympic-size swimming pool, Bill. Go shoot hoops on your indoor Staples Center replica basketball court. Go order a hooker or two and remember what your life could have been had we not made it to 100 episodes.

—Gold

Ari—

Stop writing "Gold," you incredibly pompous jackass. I write sophisticated pilots, pilots that the New York

Times *said, and I'm quoting, "...are shows that the UPN should kill for." The character of Steve Urkel is a national treasure. I practically single-handedly created TGIF! This guy Lowry belittles and demeans it and is doing everything he can to try and take money out of my children and my ex-wives' mouths. You are a powerful man. I had a hand in making you such. PLEASE DO SOMETHING OR I WILL FIND SOMEONE WHO CAN.*

—Bill

Ari—

You have not written me back. Are you ignoring me? Helllooooooo......

—Bill

Ari—

I still pay commissions there, you know.

—Bill

Ari—

I knew you were a jerk from the very first day I met you. Do you think there's anybody in this town who doesn't know you mocked up that Harvard diploma at Kinko's? My fourth wife told me you tried to molest her in Echo Park the night of my Showtime premiere. You are an animal. How do you sleep at night? A man who lives off the talents of others with no discernible talents of his own is no man at all. YOU MAKE ME SICK AND I WISH YOU AND YOUR FAMILY NOTHING BUT MISERY.

—BILL

Bickley—

Once you go after my family you've gone too far. You were a friend, and I was connected at the networks. That's why they got sold. BECAUSE OF ME! Not because of your writing. Now you may be asking yourself, How did they both go so long? I brought in a second writer who helped you turn those pieces into the successes they became. Jake Greene was my client, who I begged to do it. HE THOUGHT THEY SUCKED. But he did it because I asked him to. Oddly enough, he's had four hit shows since then and you have had none. Doesn't that tell you something? So not only should you be thanking your lucky stars for the 200-million-dollar payday you got but you should be KISSING MY ASS every chance you get. Now, Bill, I hate critics like Brian Lowry just like you do. But I don't go after them. I pity them for where they've found themselves.

—GOLD

Ari—

My show has been cancelled.

—Bill

Ari—

    It's been six months, Ari. Are you not talking to me?

—Bill

Ari—

    If this is his assistant reading this, has Ari Gold left the biz? I didn't read anything in the trades.

—Bill

Ari—

    I've got a great pilot and I've got Courteney Cox attached.

—Bill

Bill—

    Send it over and stay gold.

—Gold

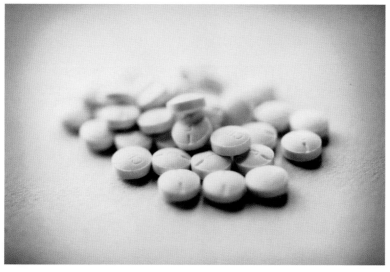

Ritalin. They tried subduing my Goldness with this when I was a kid. Instead, I turned a tidy profit and launched my career as an entrepreneur.

My strategy with Chantelle led me to banging the entire cheerleading squad.

Chess club at Harvard was a good discipline. Checkmate, bitch!

The hallway of my Michigan dorm. Some important lessons were learned here.

J. Edgar Hoover. This look says, "I own you!" Information is power, and you don't have to dress like a woman to understand that.

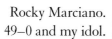

Rocky Marciano. 49–0 and my idol.

Napoleon and Genghis Khan. I keep these portraits on my bedroom wall to remind myself that I am a conqueror and a great lover.

Some Nobel laureates. I hired the four guys in the middle to dance at my son's bar mitzvah.

Vince and I. Taking over the world, together.

Lloyd. The only one who understood what it is that we really sell.

With Mark on our way to Sun Valley, where deals awaited.

The Presa Canario. This breed fought alongside Roman soldiers and can weigh up to 130 pounds. I spent a night in a cage with one so that it would never forget my scent and know that I am its master.

Meeting Queen Elizabeth before the party with ScarJo and Tony Blair. A night to remember.

Toasting with Michelle at the White House correspondents dinner. They're good sports.

This is the view from my villa on the Amalfi coast. You know what
I'd rather do than look at this all day? Make money.

PART III

ARMY

RULE #13

Sign the Circle

"You can't fuck the prom queen until she finds out her best friend jerked you off underneath the bleachers."

As a young nobody in the mailroom at TMA, I realized that the best way to accelerate my career would be to work directly for Terrance McQuewick himself. I made a point of befriending his assistant at the time and making sure that any Terrance-related errands were kicked my way. As a result, I began making weekly deliveries to Terrance's estate in Bel Air, which is where I met his second wife, a silicone-enhanced Scandinavian giraffe named Brianna.

Brianna was very beautiful, very rich, and very bored. A former development executive, she was taking some time off from work to raise their two young children (and by that I mean she played tennis every morning, drank three chardonnays with lunch at the Ivy, and had two full-time nannies at her disposal) and missed the excitement of pretending to have artistic taste. She was from the Midwest and loved talking about hockey, summers at the lake, and other reminiscences from her "authentic" childhood. During my third package run to the house, Brianna found out that I grew up in Illinois and immediately pulled me inside for a chat. From that point forward, my deliveries took a minimum of ninety minutes. Brianna kept secrets like Taylor Swift keeps boyfriends, and I quickly learned everything about Terrance McQuewick's personal life—the jealousy he felt toward his older brother, Neville, a member of British Parliament; the suspected affair with his *ex-wife*, Patrice, a repugnant trial attorney (Brianna was certain Patrice had something big on Terrance relating to his early days in business, à la Christopher Plummer in *Inside Man*); Terrance's troubling suite of sexual animal fetishes.

I didn't bang Brianna McQuewick, though (obviously) I could have. She liked to answer the door in her sports bra and vacuum-packed short-shorts, claiming I had surprised her in the middle of a workout even though her hair was perfect and she wore full makeup. Additionally, the neighborhood security guard gave her a five-minute heads-up when I came over and she always made me wait another ten at the front door. Once inside, she flirted with me like a young actress making no bones about the fact that she was willing to do whatever it took to land a supporting role on *Californication*.

"See? And they feel real, too. C'mon, give 'em a squeeze."

Tempted as I was to plow the boss's field, I tactfully slipped Brianna's advances. Our relationship was about accelerating my quest to the top, and no hero has ever benefited from fucking a Siren. That said, I did let Brianna set me up on a blind

date with one of the nannies, an aspiring ballet dancer named
Portia. It was a trap, of course. Even though we weren't hooking up, I was still having an emotional affair with Brianna,
and had I drilled the nanny, Madam McQuewick would surely
have sent us both to the guillotine. I assumed (correctly) that
Brianna was merely using Portia as her proxy for the Ari Gold
experience. As such, I treated the evening as a showcase for my
greatest hits—chef's table at the Polo Lounge followed by rooftop dancing at the Fairmont and a barefoot stroll on the beach
to end the night.

Poor Portia. She was in love before we left the restaurant
and was visibly shaken when I declined her offer to get naked
and re-create the "Wicked Game" video in the Santa Monica
surf at 3 a.m. Brianna, on the other hand, was delighted by my
beat-by-beat recounting of the date the following week.

A few months later, when Terrance's assistant was promoted to coordinator, Brianna told her husband that if he
didn't hire Ari Gold, he would be sleeping in the poolhouse for
the foreseeable future.

In those days, new agency hires were supposed to stay in the
mailroom for a minimum of one year before being considered
for promotion, but TMA made an exception for me. I remember being called up to Terrance's office like it was yesterday.

"You signed my wife, you slimy little shit." Terrance
couldn't contain his amusement. "I respect the move."

From that point forward I became Terrance McQuewick's
favored lieutenant.

Sign the Circle. I landed my first clients the same
way I bagged my boss, by "signing" their friends, relatives,

bartenders, and in-laws. I signed Alec Baldwin by helping Stephen Baldwin get cast in *Threesome* and tossing Daniel Baldwin a Pringles commercial. I signed Denise Richards after first helping her mother secure permit parking for her Beverly Hills–adjacent neighborhood. By the time my future clients met me, they had no reservations about my character or abilities because their due diligence had already been knocked out by friends and family. They trusted me and felt comfortable getting right down to business.

RULE #14

Be an Octopus at an Orgy

"You deal with talent the same way that you deal with women. You have to make them believe that they need you more than you need them."

When I worked as an assistant at TMA, one of the rising stars in the company, Brooke Devlin, invited me to a full-blown Hollywood sex party. At least, I am fairly certain that she was responsible for the invitation finding its way to my desk. Brooke was thirty-four years old and had a legendary appetite for power and sex, though most of the rumors concerning her libido were just that. No one at TMA could substantiate the myths, which is not that every agent with a package didn't try to deliver. Devlin must have been propositioned four or five times a day, but she was too smart to shit where she ate. She knew that her untouchable reputation is what drove the demand, a demand that served her career too well to risk compromise with an interoffice tryst. Devlin relished her ability to toy with and tease the weaker-minded males in the office, regaling them with stories of exotic conquests as though she were a member of their fraternity, knowing all the while that any one of them would murder the others for a chance to get in her pants.

Devlin made it known that she liked younger men, their virility, their eagerness, their willingness to learn, and I was hyperaware of her taste for veal when I was transferred in to be her assistant.

She was a consummate professional during business hours. She was neither friendly nor unfriendly, and she didn't beat around the bush when it came to delivering criticism. My biggest issue, she said, was that I had difficulty multitasking. An assistant's primary responsibility is handling phone and email traffic. You are basically air traffic control for the agent you assist. Devlin's critique of me was that I spent too much time with some flights while letting other planes crash into the ocean. She didn't offer any advice on how I could do my job better; she just told me to figure it out. Then—and this is where it gets interesting—she said, "I can tell you've got rhythm. But you need to learn how to grind." The metaphor wasn't totally on point, but it was packaged with the fact that Devlin leaned down to my desk (peek-a-boob) when she delivered the message. I took her words to heart, and to sleep, and to the shower…

The unmarked manila envelope arrived on Friday night. Devlin had asked me to stay late because she was expecting a phone call that never came. I left my desk for all of four minutes to use the bathroom and get coffee, but when I came back the envelope was there with no sign of a messenger. Inside there was a note that was empty save the following message: "11:30 p.m. Your admission is contingent on your silence."

There was a residential address listed. And there was a mask.

The address led me deep into the labyrinth of the Hollywood Hills. Keep in mind that this was before GPS, so I never really had any idea whether or not I was driving in the right direction until I reached a guard gate, where they asked to see the mask. The house that matched the address was at the end of a long driveway and there was a for-sale sign by the curb.

I was uncomfortable from the moment I walked in. The masks stayed on, but that was it. Most young guys love to talk a big game about their sexual prowess, and I was no different. However, faced with an endless pile of privates, I was totally overwhelmed. Fact is, I'm a control freak, and I wasn't comfortable with the setup. There were just too many bodies, too much traffic, and not nearly enough time or available details to control the situation. But that didn't matter once *she* found me.

I can't say for certain that the woman who "educated" me over the next forty-five minutes was Brooke Devlin (no words were spoken, the woman I was with wore colored contacts, and every identifiable mark on her body would never again be accessible for viewing), but it just made too much sense. It wasn't so much the physical aspect of the evening that made me believe I was engaging in unspeakable carnal acts with my boss, but rather the epiphanies I gleaned about customer service. More specifically, the mystery woman seemed to be leading me through a series of sexual metaphors about the following ways to best service multiple clients at once.

Respond Quickly and Defer Attention. You can't meet every need or desire as it crosses your desk (or, in the case of the orgy, the pillow grotto), but you can let clients know that you've seen their signals and then assure them that all their needs will be addressed at a later time. In the age of immediate connectivity, absence does not make the heart grow fonder; absence breeds resentment. The key is to train your clients (or your anonymous sex friends) when to call out your name.

Be Present in the Moment. Whether you are bouncing back and forth between client calls or stacked like lunchmeat in a pile of naked Hollywood executives, the pace, distraction, and noise of your environment can make it very difficult to genuinely connect with any one person. When you do make eye contact, ensure that the connection is intense and genuine enough that the person on the other end of your gaze doesn't think about the location of your other hand.

At the height of my agency career, I was actively managing roughly fifty clients. All of them were A-list earners. My core responsibility to my business was to make each client feel as though I cared about her or him more than the rest of my roster combined. I began meetings in focus and I ended meetings before that focus waned so as not to undercut the strength of my connection.

The foundation of every meaningful business relationship is trust. Trust is forged face-to-face, when a client can look me in the face and know that I give a shit. My business performance has always served to strengthen my relationships, but I made it my mission to convince myself, and thus my clients, that my purpose in life was to keep them satisfied and exceed their needs.

"Servicing" Customers vs. Customer Service. Hookers, Hondas, and Hollywood all approach customers with a different mindset than the rest of the business world. Whereas most businesses talk about the importance of "customer service," agents, mechanics, and people of the night talk about "servicing customers." It is an important distinction, as customer service is generally a reactive process in which professionals and businesses responds to the needs of their clients, while servicing customers involves exploration to discover what the customer needs in order to start firing on all cylinders. Clients and customers might think they know what they need, but you will likely uncover several ailments and opportunities once you probe under the hood or, in the case of my Hollywood Hills evening, the taint.

The masked woman who may or may not have been my boss was excruciatingly slow, beautifully deliberate. She was like a point guard reining in the flow of a basketball game, surveying the court and identifying strategies to break down the defense. She made me stop thinking about my needs and start feeling them. I was so consumed by her genius. What I thought I wanted and needed heading into that experience was totally different than what I actually required to reach the next level of performance.

To clarify, I did not immediately recognize the business applications of my experience as I slid around the terra cotta tiles of that house in the hills, lubed up like a human prisoner in *The Matrix*. My epiphany came weeks later at work. My personal and professional thoughts finally cross-pollinated when Devlin, who had treated me with complete indifference since that special night, complimented me on my multitasking.

"I think you're finally getting the hang of this."

"Well, I had a good teacher."

Devlin smirked. I was transferred off of her desk the next day, but my clients have benefited from her teaching ever since. Eventually my wife reaped the rewards as well.

RULE #15

Tell the Important Part of the Truth

*"Expectations, you beat 'em by a dollar, life is great.
Get under by a dollar, put a gun in your mouth and
make sure I'm standing behind you."*

Had I never become a Hollywood agent I would have made a hell of a hedge fund manager, raising money from extremely wealthy people, packaging assets for investment, and then distracting regulators when they inquired about the origins of my fantastic wealth. Great hedge fund managers operate like elite NFL quarterbacks, popping Oxy like Mentos before analyzing the playing field for leverage to exploit. More importantly, both QBs and fund managers reserve the right to call audibles at the line of scrimmage. I do the same thing with feature film projects. I package the initial talent and resources to get a project off the ground and then immediately start changing the plays. The package you see on-screen—actors, directors, locations, even the stories—almost never resembles the portfolio I initially sell to investors, which is fine as long as everybody makes enough money to upgrade their penthouses in Cabo.

I never lie to my investors. I simply protect them from their own ignorance. Captains of finance and technology want to believe that they can conquer any industry with formulas and algorithms. Unfortunately, Hollywood isn't like other industries. Algorithms don't do a whole lot of good when your assets enter rehab in the middle of a shoot or take off on the back of Justin Bieber's Ducati. The human element in Hollywood is more volatile than any financial variant hedge fund managers could ever dream up. Making a movie is a wild ride, and my job as a producer and agent is to keep my people on the goddamn bull. As soon as the bucking starts, all rules are out the window, which is why I never make promises. Instead, I simply state my intentions, thereby leaving the door open for dramatic and inevitable change.

About twenty years ago, I was asked to raise money for *American Pie*, which needed about twelve million dollars to get off of life support. One of my buddies from business school, Brian Padrez, had been bugging me for years about wanting to invest in Hollywood, and this project seemed like the perfect opportunity for a self-described "really funny guy" like Brian, so I met him at his house in Woodland Hills. Brian is an incredibly smart guy, and he made a fortune in the insurance business, but as far as Hollywood was concerned he was "dumb money." He knew nothing about riding the bull. Hollywood runs on dumb money from smart people, and managing dumb money investors has always been one of my specialties because I know how to service both their intellect and their vanity.

Brian, like most wealthy investors, had a lot of non-negotiables for his money during that first meeting in Woodland Hills: He didn't want any nudity in "his" movie, he wanted James Van Der Beek to be the star, and he wanted me to promise that I wouldn't come back to him for more money in the middle of production. If I could guarantee those three points, he'd cut me a check. I said I'd do my best, knowing full well that all three non-negotiables would be in play sooner rather than later. Non-negotiables during production are just like non-negotiables during sex—you can run red lights in the name of passion as long as you don't kill the vibe by asking for permission.

Nudity was first. If you want a little comedy to make big money, the yellow brick road should be paved with gratuitous tits. From Jamie Lee Curtis in *Trading Places* to Phoebe Cates in *Fast Times at Ridgemont High*, cinematic history is overflowing with examples of A and B comedies that have been enhanced by C- and D-cups. Today even more so, as Chinese men troll through videos like teenagers at Blockbuster in the nineties, hunting for credible titles with incredible titties so they can get aroused without arousing the suspicion of the women in their households. Anyhow, Brian said "nudity" was off-limits, which I decided to interpret as "totally naked," meaning T&A was okay so long as we kept the babymakers out of the frame. I had another one of the producers, David Bertin, call Brian and explain the artistic importance of showing raw passion on the screen. He described Shannon Elizabeth's self-stimulation scene like it was impressionist masterpiece and not simply a Playmate with a bad accent double-clicking her mouse.

The "more money" call was next. Technically, I never asked Brian for more cash. Instead, I just talked to him about some cool shit we could never possibly afford. Rich men are like little boys in that they are drawn to everything that has been deemed off-limits. They don't like being told they can't have every toy on the shelf. Despite my (mock) protests, Brian commanded that I spend an additional million-five on a top-shelf special effects package.

We were never going to get James Van Der Beek. We didn't have the budget and, more importantly, VDB was booked out three years in advance. I knew that Brian would be disappointed, so I needed to accompany the bad news with a miracle. I called Brian a week after our Woodland Hills meeting with an exciting development: We had tentative deals in place with Lebowski's slutty wife and the Jewish kid from *Angels in the Outfield* for a fraction of their normal rates! There was one problem, though. Van Der Beek was booked solid. I told Brian that VDB adored *American Pie* and would love to do it when *Varsity Blues* wrapped, but that meant we would have to cut our other stars loose and accept that they would likely be out of our price range by the time we got back into production. If there's one thing rich guys hate more than being told they can't have something, it's being told they have to wait. Even so, I was amazed at the speed with which Brian Padrez kicked his VDB ambitions to the curb for Tara Reid. Meanwhile, I was excited that two of my young clients were finally getting decent work.

Successfully managing investors starts with managing their expectations and ends by ensuring a satisfactory return on their investment. If you make money, your investors will shut up and write you another check. If you lose money, you had better have an alternative vanity-driven ROI waiting in the wings. If you can't make your investors wealthier, you can make them cooler by setting up some cocaine-fueled celebrity playdates in Vegas or ensuring that your shitty movie has an epic premiere and after-party. Rich people have no problem dumping small fortunes into a great party or a great story. Why else would venture capitalists willingly pay twenty grand to dry hump Ke$ha's backup dancers in a booth filled with thirty-dollar bottles of Three Olives at Hakkasan? Give your dumb money investors the executive producer treatment and they'll never cut off your credit.

Earlier in this book, I discussed the importance of manufacturing heat as a means for creating external market demand. Heat is equally essential when separating rich people from their hard-inherited cash, and the fastest way to turn on the furnace is by pushing two buttons that I alluded to briefly in the preceding story: scarcity and urgency.

Scarcity. Rich people get off on possessing one-of-a-kind items that are unavailable to other rich people. I have a hookup at Tesla Motors and was one of the first people in Southern California to get a Model S. For weeks, people stopped me in the middle of North Canon Drive to take pictures with my car as the biggest hitters in town watched enviously with mouths full of eggs Benedict from Porta Via. I shit you not, I was driving through Beverly Hills with Joey Boukadakis sitting shotgun when a TMZ bus pulled up next to us at a stoplight and not one of the overweight Nebraskans on board noticed the Academy Award–winning director!

When I initially went to pick up my Tesla, I brought a rich friend of mine, Paul James, to the dealership (which hadn't officially opened yet). When we were growing up in Chicago, Paul ran diamonds for the mafia, and by twenty he was running his own crews out of a Gold Coast penthouse. At twenty-eight he was a few moves away from a federal indictment when I introduced him to the writers of an indie script called *The Blair Witch Project*. He turned twenty grand into twenty million, moved out to Hollywood, and became a real-life Chili Palmer. Ten years later Paul was worth nine figures.

When we rolled into the Tesla dealership there were only two cars on the property, my car and a tricked-out concept model. Naturally, Paul eyed the concept.

"How much?"

"That car is not for sale, sir," the salesman told Paul. "It's a concept car. The materials used in the frame of that automobile are too expensive for mass production. The battery alone would cost over two hundred thousand dollars."

"How much?"

"Sir, I'm sorry. I can't sell you this car. And even if I could it would be at least six hundred thousand dollars."

I turned to Paul and offered him my new car for fifty grand above the sticker price, but he now had his heart set on the unattainable concept model.

We picked up my car and drove to the Soho House for lunch. The valets in the garage went nuts, taking pictures and celebrating as if El Tri had just won the World Cup. Paul pouted like a six-year-old until he pulled out his cell phone and called the Tesla salesman.

"If you can have that car at the Soho House valet by the time I finish my Scotch, I'll give you seven fifty in cash."

Paul got the car and Tesla got an extra buck fifty.

Urgency. Rich investors and executives are horrified by the thought of being last. They are the parents who break out in hives on December 20 when they realize that several houses on their block already have a Tickle Me Elmo under the tree.

Ten years ago, Jason Lee was up for the lead in a network sitcom pilot called *My Name Is Earl* about a trailer-trash alcoholic who decides to right the wrongs of his pathetic past. Jason had breezed through the callbacks and killed his camera test in front of the producers, and my sources told me that he was one of three finalists for the gig. My job, at that point, was to make sure that Jason became Tickle Me Elmo in the minds of the showrunners. Problem was, he was the least famous of the three finalists vying for the role. The other two guys were talentless cadavers ten years too old to play the effervescent white-trash lead, but that didn't matter because Hollywood executives are notoriously lazy and short-sighted when it comes to casting (see: Tom Cruise as Jack Reacher).

Studio execs play not to lose, like gazelles sprinting furiously around a watering hole but never daring to jump in. They prefer the safety of the herd to the risk (and possible reward) of being first. In this case, my boy, J Lee, was the oasis. He was an obvious stud with great comedic timing and an everyman vibe. Sure, he wasn't good-looking, and he still carried the low-budget stench of Kevin Smith projects, but his indie past certainly should have trumped the Betty Ford experiences of the other two guys. The executives continued to flinch, however, because Jason Lee had never carried a show, and they were scared to go first.

My job was to show them that they weren't first.

I used the same technique to get Kevin Jonas cast in Ang Lee's Genghis Khan biopic. The financiers wanted Nick and Joe, the two younger Jonas brothers, to play Western-born monks in the film. Joe, fresh off doing jack shit, was in. Nick, on the other hand, had become a pop star and was completely off-limits, but did I tell the financiers that? Of course not. I told them that Kevin, the older, awkward, married Jonas brother, was out of their reach. Joe and Nick could make it work, but Kevin was going to get Oscar buzz for his upcoming portrayal of young John Travolta in *A Man Confused*, and even if Kevin's schedule opened up, he would be way out of their price range. The financiers refused to take no for an answer and ended up paying Kevin triple his quote.

I never had any intention of dating Chantelle Foster, but after we hooked up I made sure she felt appreciated and important, and, more importantly, made sure that the other girls saw her feeling appreciated and important. I had "anonymous" flowers delivered to her at cheerleading practice even though their origin would be obvious. I even leveraged my position as the student council president to get Chantelle a universal hall pass, a laminated card that afforded her safe passage throughout the hallways during school hours. I wanted the other girls to know that hooking up with Ari Gold would improve their lives. While the jocks were fighting over who had the biggest cock, I was gobbling up all the free agents because they wanted the lifestyle afforded by my companionship.

I signed Cuba Gooding Jr. the same way.

In 1995, I was one of a dozen people in a meeting with Cuba at TMA. As one of the biggest stars in Hollywood at the time, Cuba had the ability to chart his own course through Hollywood. After the success of *Boyz n the Hood*, he had his eye on meatier roles, and we were all called to the conference room to pitch projects for him. Most of the scripts tossed around in that meeting were generic urban dramas that had already been turned down by Will Smith. Worse, the point person on Cuba's agency team, Adam Cozad, had done little to no curation ahead of time, which meant that not only were the projects dogshit, but they also were totally off-genre. Cuba listened patiently to each horrid idea, though his attention visibly waned as the meeting wore on. By the time the meeting ended and Cozad was declaring victory, Cuba was ready to jump to CAA. He wasn't about to suffer through another *Lightning Jack*. Luckily I stepped in and dusted off my Chantelle Foster routine.

As chance would have it, Cuba was leaving the next day for Alabama, where he was starring in a war epic, *The Tuskegee Airmen*, that was being directed by one of my early clients, Robert Markowitz. Marko wasn't exactly a tentpole client for my young book of business, but with Cuba in the neighborhood I decided that my boy, Bob, needed a little TLC. I flew east and drove down to the set, a good four hours from civilization, where the air is so heavy and you get so sweaty that if you walk more than a block you start to feel like you've got a porn star riding on your shoulders. Markowitz was totally confused by my presence, and I didn't waste any time explaining myself to him except to say that I wanted to check in and drop off some Pappy Van Winkle to help make the boondocks feel a little more like home. Then I went to look for Cuba.

Cuba Gooding Jr. is a method actor, which means that he inhabits his characters wholly and completely, adopting their mannerisms and attitudes regardless of whether or not the cameras are rolling. As such, he is supposed to be completely off-limits to people like me when he is on set. I waited to make my move until the cast and crew broke for dinner. Cuba chose to hang back and use the time to break down and reassemble his rifle. What a pro.

"Cuba!"

He looked up, clearly not recognizing me.

"Ari Gold. We met in the meeting at TMA. I was the only guy *not* pitching you *Boyz Back n the Hood*."

That broke the ice. He smiled and asked me what I was doing so far from LA, and I told him about Marko. Cuba was clearly impressed by my client service commitment and was even more impressed when I pulled out the folder I had brought for him. The folder was labeled CUBA OSCAR PROJECTS and contained roughly nine hundred blank pieces of paper. I hadn't yet found the right scripts for Cuba, but I was betting that he wouldn't want the folder around to distract him from his military duties.

"When I found out you and Marko were working together

on this project, I put together a sampling of material I thought you might respond to."

"Thanks, Ari. I'll take a look." He took the folder from me, and for a brief moment I saw my abbreviated career flash before my eyes. Luckily he passed it back. "On second thought, let's just grab lunch when I'm back in LA and you can talk me through the highlights."

Four weeks later, Cuba Gooding Jr. and I had lunch at the Beverly Hills Hotel and I walked him through three promising feature film scripts, one of which, *Jerry Maguire*, would become the high point of his career (at least until *Boat Trip*).

■ GOLD NUGGET ■
HONE YOUR LIP SERVICE LISTENING

One of my clients, an iconic action star from the eighties who shall remain nameless, was in Vancouver a couple years ago to shoot a Jackie Chan kung fu piece of shit. Two days before production, my client calls to tell me that he doesn't want his character to die in the film. Dying doesn't fit his "brand," and he wants the studio to change the ending of the script. Keep in mind, my guy was getting paid $5 million to be the bad guy in this movie and he only had to work for six days. There was no way in hell the studio was going to change the ending, but did I tell my client that? Of course not. I told my HGH-ingesting, hair-plugged, has-been client that I fought the studio and forced them to rewrite act 3. However, in order to make things work with the production schedule, they wouldn't be able to shoot the new ending until the rest of the film was wrapped, which meant that my guy would have to stay in Canada for an extra three weeks if he wanted his character to live.

Actors will fight for their integrity only so long as it doesn't fuck with their vacation time. Faced with the prospect of having to delay a tantric weekend at Amangiri with his Bollywood girlfriend, my guy chose to die in that movie with a grateful goddamn smirk on his face. He just wanted to know that someone was listening.

RULE #16

Housebreak Your Subordinates

"You ungrateful piece of shit!
Ari Gold made your career!"

Surround yourself with the best people and make sure they know that you're better than they are. I train my people like I have my personal assistant train my dogs: to please, play, and protect.

PLEASE. I have a well-earned reputation for being aggressive in groups. I yell, threaten, taunt, and publicly shame with uncommon enthusiasm. Yet, throughout my tenure as an agency head, my employees never rebelled in protest of my direct leadership style. Instead they used my fire as motivation to be better than the overachiever sitting next to them. None of my agents felt threatened by my rants because they each had private and unique personal relationships with me, as though I was the patriarch of a polygamist family in which each agent was an obedient wife.

When we were alone, I made sure that each of my people understood why I believed he or she was special, and as a result each was determined to please me in his or her own unique way in order to create separation from the less-favored wives. When I lost my temper in the conference room, each agent would smirk at the others as if to say, "I knew this was coming. We talked about it on my special night."

The key to maintaining family harmony in my Utah-pian metaphor was ensuring that each of my lieutenants possessed unique skills and responsibilities and therefore felt productive in ways that would not be threatened by the success of the others. My sensible and organized wife took pride in his operational predictability and consistency, while my freaky youngest wife reveled in the opportunity to seek out more spontaneous methods for growing the business.

PLAY. The strongest companies throw the best parties. Fun and loyalty are intertwined in the millennial marketplace, which is why Google pays hundreds of thousands of dollars flying in European DJs to spin for the gaggle of socially inept computer nerds at their Christmas party. Thing is, agents need to play on a daily basis. Computer geeks are like English Bulldogs. They'll run around for a few minutes, get overwhelmed, and then fall asleep in their own stink. Agents are like Weimaraners. They can chase down a tennis ball for thirty-six-hour stretches and still show up perky for work on Monday. When I founded MGA, I saw a huge opportunity to take over the "play" space, which is why I developed the MGA Omnicard.

Instead of simply passing out ID cards to employees, I gave every MGA employee a key to the city in the form of a credit card. The Omnicards were all black, save the small MGA logo inlaid in fourteen-karat gold. The cards were impressively heavy, like the rectangular gambling chips in Monte Carlo casinos, but far more valuable than cash because the Omnicards ensured access to every desirable space in Hollywood. Before issuing the cards, I had one of my assistants cut deals with every hot restaurant and club in Los Angeles, along with all of the major sports teams and event spaces. Basically, carrying an Omnicard was like walking around town with Gisele on your arm. Nothing was off-limits.

The cards were expensive to manufacture, and Barbara Miller nearly blew out her Depends when I told her how much we were spending on each one. Pricey as the cards were, however, the investment paid off tenfold because the status afforded to each cardholder was worth at least $60K in annual salary on the open market. The Omnicard dropped more panties than an OB-GYN. Better yet, the cards did not specify one's position within the company, which meant that the mailroom women and men were able to trade on A-list currency while making nearly minimum wage. Their gratitude hung in the atmosphere like Hong Kong smog.

PROTECT. One of the first clients that I represented as an agent was an NFL player turned comedic actor, Bob Golic. He was a mountain of a man with a taste for beer, stone-washed jeans, and a mullet that would've made Lorenzo Lamas blush. In those early years, before I had a real reputation to lean on, the personal service I offered my clients had to be second to none. I found real estate agents, tutors for their children, second husbands, and anything else that would showcase my dedication while warding off potential poachers from rival agencies. With Golic, the sharks began circling following his role as resident advisor Mike Rogers on *Saved by the Bell: The College Years*. ICM wanted him, WME wanted him, and CAA was pretending to be apathetic, which meant that they were willing to kill for him.

When Golic asked if I could pick up his new puppies from a breeder in the Valley, I cleared the time. What he failed to tell me, however, was that I wasn't going to be retrieving normal puppies like Labs or Beagles. In typical new money fashion, Golic wanted unique pets, canine symbols of strength and masculinity to make up for his waning athletic ability. Golic wanted Presa Canarios.

Presa Canarios are one of the most fearsome dog breeds on the planet. They look like the result of a hot weekend between pit bulls and African lions. Look 'em up on YouTube. They will scare the shit out of you. When I first rolled up to the breeder's compound, I didn't understand why he needed the eight-foot electric fence circling his beat-up motor home, but as soon as I saw the prehistoric jaws on one of the full-grown beasts gnawing on a Durango muffler in the yard, I got the message. Why Golic would want the monster from *Ghostbusters* growing up in his Marina Del Rey townhouse was beyond me, but my job at that point was to service, not question.

Golic called my cell as I was driving home with the pups and asked if I could keep the "lil critters" for a few nights because he wanted to ride his bike down to Laughlin and "git after it." I said fine as long as I could stay at his house with the pups. I called my assistant and had him pull some reading material on the breed.

Presa Canarios are intelligent, headstrong, ferocious, and very suspicious of strangers. Basically, they will kill for their family and they will kill strangers. If you want to be in their family, they need to learn your scent early. They also need to learn that you are in charge and that you control their food source. Those first couple nights in Marina Del Rey, I slept *in* the kennel with the pups. Even though I didn't expect their owner to have a long and illustrious acting career, I still wanted those dogs to respect the smell of Gold.

The Miller/Gold Agency was full of Presa Canario agents. My women and men were intimidating and impressive killers, but they loved me unconditionally and were willing take on a jungle full of predators in order to protect my ass. They learned my scent at an early age and understood that I was the only one who could feed them, exercise them, and allow them to hunt.

The Puppy Test. No matter how capable your people are of pleasing and protecting you, it all goes to shit if they can't be trusted to keep their emotions in check. My old contractor, Mario, was a great example. I met the guy after my wife hired him to renovate our kitchen. Roughly my age, Mario had grown up in a working-class Chicago neighborhood, and we knew some of the same people from back in the day. Mario did great work on our cabinets, and he was a fun guy to drink with, so he quickly became our "house guy." Whether we needed to patch a wall or add a second story on to our guesthouse, we called Mario. I introduced the guy around, he got a lot of business from my network, and he became a very loyal friend. What I didn't know at the time was that Mario was an emotional time bomb.

Fast forward a year and Mario was watching a Lakers/ Bulls game at Goal, an upscale sports bar in West Hollywood, when he overheard one of my former clients badmouthing me in the booth next to him. Being the loyal Presa that he was, Mario stood up on his booth cushion and went off on the guy.

"You ungrateful piece of shit! Ari Gold made your career! Was it Ari's fault that you solicited a switch-hitting underage prostitute in Mexico City when you were supposed to be in your trailer improving your ridiculous Spanish accent, you talentless pile of shit? You better shut your fuckin' mouth right now or I'll throw my knee through your fake-ass grill!"

Thank God Goal has a strict no pics/no video policy, or I would have been charged with guilt by association on TMZ for at least a week. As it was, I almost got dragged into the mess later that night when Mario continued to talk trash to the guy on Twitter. Thank God nobody pays attention to a handyman with thirteen followers.

My failure in the Mario situation was that I didn't administer a puppy test before letting him into my inner circle. I saw the please/play/protect instincts but failed to screen for crazy.

The purpose of the puppy test is to see how a given animal reacts when faced with sudden and unsettling activity. Depending on which dog website you look at, the puppy test can be administered by opening an umbrella in the dog's face, surprising the dog when it's sleeping, or simply petting the dog on the floor between your legs and watching to see if the little fucker tries to bite your ankles.

Today, I administer some form of puppy test to every person I let into my life. I pay waiters to "accidentally" pour water on potential clients during lunch at the Chateau, I kill the power during new agents' presentations, and I pay off high school referees to issue unwarranted technical fouls to the pimple-faced sophomores who try to date my daughter. You can't put a price tag on crazy.

■ GOLD NUGGET ■
NEVER BE AN ASSHOLE IN WRITING

Never rant on the record. I don't care how upset you are about employee incompetence or customer entitlement, never text or type your uncensored frustration. The executives at Sony learned this lesson for all of Hollywood when the North Koreans hacked their servers in 2014 and Amy Pascal's shit-talking emails were released to *Variety*, TMZ, and Deadline. Funny thing is, I nearly fell on that grenade several years earlier than Amy after mistakenly sending a scathing diatribe to the wrong BlackBerry.

I had a kid working for me at the time whose incompetence was both infuriating and baffling. After failing to confirm two meetings in the same day, the latter of which resulted in me driving to Tarzana, I was prepared to tie the dumb bastard's noose myself. In a fit of rage, I wrote down my uncensored opinions of the little shit and sent them to one of my partners. At least I thought that's where I was sending my rant. Only after I pushed Send did I realize that I had sent a message about strangling the kid and tossing his fat, lifeless body into the LA River to the kid himself. Had the kid been by his BlackBerry when I sent the message, he would have forwarded it on to Deadline before filing his harassment suit.

Realizing what I had done, I sprinted into the center of our office and demanded that everyone in the company stop what they were doing and immediately hand over their BlackBerrys. Our office had become too dependent on technology, I told them, and I wanted them to spend the rest of the day relearning what it meant to service our clients by interacting with them directly.

The sack-of-shit kid was in the bathroom (thank God!), so I took the BlackBerry off his desk myself as the rest of the office reluctantly handed over their devices to my assistant. At the time, BlackBerrys operated peer-to-peer, which meant that as long as I could disable his phone there would be no record of the message stored online.

I gave the dangerous BlackBerry to my kids and instructed them to total the fucking thing beyond recognition. For the next two hours, they ran over that phone with their skateboards and smashed it with hammers like it was Gallagher's watermelon, and we even played catch with its remains in my pool. It was the best family bonding we had in years.

The next day, I returned 149 BlackBerrys to their terrified owners. The exercise had rendered my people basically useless for twenty-four hours, a financial hit I was willing to endure in order to ensure the longevity of my career. Obviously, one guy didn't get his phone back. I told the kid it must have gotten lost and had my assistant go buy him a new one. To this day he has no idea that the fat, lifeless corpse of his BlackBerry is lying at the bottom of the LA River.

RULE #17

If You Don't Have Enemies, Get Some

"I don't steal other people's motherfucking clients.
But in your case, I am going to make an exception!"

Live long enough and you come to the profound yet utterly pedestrian realization that most people are pussies. They'll do anything they can to avoid conflict. You don't need a PhD in psychology to know that when put to the gauntlet, the majority of mankind would rather run and hide under their sensible Ikea bedframe than stand up and fight like a bloodthirsty conquistador sacking a city. And that's fine. We call those people employees. They are welcome to serve as our subordinates and genuflect at the altar of our magnificence. There's a reason pawns exist in a game of chess; someone has to die first.

But no man ever ascended to the throne without a few axes swung at his head. Genghis Khan didn't conquer half the known world doling out feel-good high fives and reacharounds. He did it by lighting anyone on fire who got in his way and pissing blood on their still-smoking carcasses. You don't get to storm the castle, seize the treasure, and bang the king's daughter bareback without some kind of a battle royal. We're not at fifth-grade Jewish soccer camp where everyone gets a participation trophy along with their yarmulke. The hard truth is that life is a raging sea of dicks with only so many vaginas. Those who don't make it inside the silky pink life raft fast enough have to jerk themselves off.

In your quest to rule, conflict is inevitable. The sooner you accept this, the sooner you can learn to embrace it and grow from it.

Remember that scene in *Fight Club* where Tyler Durden (Brad Pitt) tells his disciples to go out and pick a fight with someone random off the street? What was he trying to teach them?

First, that most people are inherently conflict-averse.

Second, and most important, you shouldn't shy away from conflict, but open yourself up to it. Conflict isn't a vampire. It doesn't have to be formally invited in for some foie gras and a Perrier to cross the threshold of your studio apartment—it's fucking coming in regardless. All you can control is how you choose to greet it. By cowering in fear? Or foot raised atop a wooden stump at the beach ready to deliver a crane kick like your boy Mr. Miyagi taught you?

Conflict has helped make me the man I am today. The first time I remember knowing conflict was something I wanted in my life was in kindergarten. It was show-and-tell day. We all had to bring something to class, so my mom made me bring a dreidel, as if any five-year-olds were interested in a centuries-old

Jewish gambling toy that spun for about five seconds then fell to the ground like the dumb piece of wood it was. I don't remember what everyone else brought that day except for this one kid in my class, Dick Hillenbrand, who waltzed in with the most incredible toy that, up to that point in my relatively sheltered middle-class existence, I had ever laid eyes upon. It was an awesome Godzilla doll. Two feet tall with movable plastic arms and legs, razor sharp teeth, and huge silver scales jutting out the spine and tail. Fuck, it was badass.

The rule was that when we walked in the room we had to put whatever we brought on an entryway table so we wouldn't screw around with it during our lesson. The Godzilla was instantly the envy of the room, and I was transfixed.

After what felt like an eternity, we finally got to show-and-tell. The teacher told everyone to go up to the table and bring over what they had brought. And in that moment, I came to a profound realization—the burning desire to have what I wanted was always going to trump the fear of getting in trouble for going after it. I walked up to the table, took the Godzilla toy, lifted it over my head like I'd just come down from Mount Sinai holding a stone tablet with the word of God on it, and told the class to behold that which was *mine*. The teacher didn't see what item each of us came in with, so she had no idea that it didn't belong to me. Needless to say, Dick Hillenbrand went fucking crazy, calling me a liar, rightfully claiming the toy to be his, and so forth. Everything he argued against me sent an electric charge through my prepubescent body that day. It sparked something inside of me—it gave me a voice. In that instant, at five years old, Ari Gold's love for conflict was born. What happened next I barely remember because I must have blacked out for a second, but I delivered one of the most powerful, impassioned diatribes of my five-year-old life, shaming Dick for having the gall and audacity to claim what was so obviously my Godzilla doll as his. Right there on the spot I created an entire backstory for the toy, including what kind of cereal I had on the day my parents bought it for me. By the end of it, I think I had convinced myself that I really *did* own the Godzilla. Regardless, it was enough to convince my teacher, who believed me over Dick and let me go home with the toy. Dick had to take the dreidel. Kid wasn't even Jewish. I kept Godzilla on my nightstand like a trophy. (Ironically, years later Dick became a billionaire by investing in JDate, the Jewish dating website, among other tech companies. When I'm in Chicago and happen to drive by his $20 million estate in Highland Park, sometimes I think, "Man, maybe I shouldn't have stolen his fucking Godzilla...")

I learned that not only could I benefit from welcoming conflict, but there was something to be said for sparking it.

Now, I'm not telling you to go start shit with your mailman or accountant or manicurist, but if you start leaning into the punches life throws at you as opposed to rearing back from them, you'll be surprised how much better of a position you're in to counterattack with an uppercut versus a bitch-slap. If you can master that which most people fear—the fear of conflict—then you're light years ahead of the game. So take arms, soldier, and dive headfirst into the fray like you're storming the beaches at Normandy and go slaughter some metaphorical Nazis.

While conflict is a constant in our lives, this chapter is also about that which is spawned from its fiery, unwieldy, iron-wrought bowels: *Enemies.*

Most people think they don't want enemies. They systematically wish to be liked by everyone. Maybe that works if you're a twenty-four-year-old kindergarten teacher with D-cups and a closet full of cropped knit sweaters, but for the rest of the human race, it's a naïve approach to take. We don't live in a utopian society inspired by a gay marriage between Mr. Rogers and Barney. It's not called *The Plenty of Food for Everyone Games.* Enemies exist, and they're an important part of the game board. You need to learn how to smoke them out and play them for your benefit, or you will get crushed.

There's an old maxim that says, "When the student is ready, the master will appear." (Proof—you picked up this book and, shazaam, here I am, bitch!) Correspondingly, I would add, "When an enemy appears, you're doing something right." Or the reverse: "If you don't have enemies, you're doing something wrong."

I've had countless enemies over the years. But one of my most memorable was this kid in high school named David Ready. Ready was this six-foot-tall mongoloid bruiser who looked more like he should have been playing on the defensive line for the Bears than repeating his junior year as a transfer student at Roosevelt High. He would go around school giving anyone who looked at him the wrong way a "shit mustache," sticking his finger up his own ass then smearing it across some unsuspecting kid's upper lip.

On his first day of school he started dating this girl, Kate Herman, who we'd all known since we were kids. For whatever reason Ready decided he didn't like the idea of her having ever dated anyone else, so this lunatic starts going around the school kicking the shit out of anyone who had ever so much as held hands with her since the first grade. Kate was a bit of a slut, so that was practically half of our entire class. And unfortunately for me, I was the guy who took her virginity freshman year in the backseat of her family Astro van while her mom was inside shopping at Target.

Once Ready found that out, he wanted nothing more than to kill my scrawny Jew ass. He would walk up and down the halls telling the world he was going to murder my face, my body, and end my entire bloodline.

Now, I'm all for having enemies, but at two hundred pounds with anger issues and an ax to grind, this was a pretty fucking big enemy.

There's no way I could have taken him physically, so I knew I had to get creative.

In circumstances such as these, your best bet is to try to flip an enemy into an ally. This is traditionally accomplished in one of two ways: either by finding a common enemy to align against, or by offering your enemy something they want more than your demise. Ready and I didn't have a common enemy, but there was one thing that he, and every other guy with eyes and a functioning dick in the school wanted, that I was in a unique position to facilitate.

Her name was Ms. Teifeld, and she was the school's new librarian. At age twenty-three, she had recently graduated from Notre Dame and had decided to spend a couple of years working in the public education system before going to law school. A buxom redhead with curves for days, she made Joan's double-Ds on *Mad Men* look like negligible mosquito bites. You couldn't help but find yourself drifting into the library under the guise of messing around on the microfiche machine just to get a glimpse of her cleavage as she bent down to restock books in the nonfiction section.

Because I was a junior, I got to choose an elective that year, and in my infinite wisdom I chose to be a library aide, knowing I wouldn't really have to do anything, using that time as office hours to run my various businesses and take meetings with students who worked for me. Ms. Teifeld started after I was already an aide, so her tits were just an added bonus.

Ms. Teifeld, or Tammy, as she asked me to call her when no one else was around, had recently gone through a short-lived marriage and a rocky divorce. She was tired of men who didn't appreciate her and at a point in her life where she just wanted to blow off some steam and have fun.

It was clear from the start that there was one thing Ms. Teifeld needed more than anything else.

A fuck buddy.

She even shared with me once that one of her fantasies was sleeping with a student in the book stacks. And while I had hoped to slide myself into that position, I realized this was a chip I could play to potentially turn that animal Ready to my side.

When you're a teenage boy, the only thing better than banging an adult woman is banging an adult woman who works at your high school.

I caught Ready off guard in the parking lot one afternoon.

As he was getting into his car, I slipped into the passenger seat.

"Look, man, I know you want to kick my teeth in, but I've got something you'll want much more: the chance to be a legend."

I think he was so stunned by the balls it took to confront him like that, he listened to what I had to say and, as I hoped he would be, was partial to my plan versus smashing my head through his front windshield.

Smartly, I'd been priming the pump with Ms. Teifeld for a full week, telling her about this incredibly mature student named David Ready, talking him up, hammering home how good he was at discretion, how he would be a perfect candidate for her fantasy liaison, etc.

(If this is starting to sound like something out of *Penthouse Letters*, you're right. I sent the story in and was proud to find it published in the April 1982 issue.)

So I arranged for Ms. Teifeld to conveniently be "working" Saturday afternoon at the school library, right at the same time Ready was finishing with wrestling practice. The rest was up to them. Turns out, for as big of a meathead as he was, Ready knew how to handle older women. And he handled Ms. Teifeld all the way from the reference section to the geography section and up and back again multiple times over.

My enemy had become my ally.

He became a legend. I didn't get killed. And in the end, we became friends. He was my protector through the rest of high school, saving my ass numerous times over. No one got hurt in this charade of mine, except for Kate, who Ready immediately broke up with in order to keep fucking Ms. Teifeld.

No one in school could understand how all of a sudden this guy who wanted to destroy me had overnight practically become my personal security and lapdog.

I never said a word about it until now, in turn increasing my own legend as well. That's the power of a good enemy.

Enemies, archenemies, rivals—from my perspective, they're all the same thing. Someone coming after your cheese. If you're out there making waves in the world, trust me, you won't have to find them, they'll find you.

I think Eminem by way of Winston Churchill said it best, "It's good to have enemies. It means you've stood for something." Hear, hear. Would love to see a hologram of the old British PM rapping that line onstage with Slim Shady at Coachella next year, Tupac-style.

Bottom line, here's what you need to know: Every powerful person has enemies. If you want to achieve greatness, you need them, too.

Why exactly do you need enemies? Why does Sherlock Holmes need Moriarty? Ali need Frazier? Superman need Lex Luthor? Magic need Bird? Coke need Pepsi? Seinfeld need Newman? Jesus need the Jews? Because they push one another to be *better*. To go beyond their own limitations. To become greater than they thought possible. People always say to seek out mentors. Sometimes a worthy adversary can be just as effective. There is no stronger motivator for self-improvement than the knowledge that, right now, at this very moment, someone or some group of someones is out there in the world training, grinding, masterminding—employing every resource at their disposal and weapon in their arsenal—to try to take you down, vaporize your existence, and annihilate everything you have so carefully and methodically built.

When I was running the Miller/Gold Agency, the largest, most successful agency in Hollywood at the time, I woke up every single morning at 5 a.m. in my one-thousand-thread-count Egyptian cotton sheets, lying beside a peacefully dreaming Mrs. Ari, listening to the tranquil fountain in the outside foyer of my Brentwood mansion, alert with the sobering, gut-punching, stark awareness that enemies—some obvious in the clear light of day, others more opaque and lurking in the shadows—were gunning to obliterate my name and my business. They wanted to destroy me. And you know what? I liked it. Not at first, but I taught myself to. Over time I learned to not only embrace it, but to *need* it. That feeling of "fight or die" lit a fire under me, incited me to seek out and become the best version of myself. I knew that if I slipped up, made a mistake, exposed a weakness, had too many blind spots, moved too early or too late—or committed any other number of countless miscalculations or oversights—there were barbarians with battle-axes and flamethrowers waiting at the gate, champing at the bit to make me eat a made-to-order shit sandwich, charbroiled and well done. And while we want our enemies to come from the quality of work we do, in reality, they can come from almost anywhere. Which is why you need to have eyes in the back of your head with 20/20 vision and infrared night goggles.

It sounds counterintuitive to say, but you need to recalibrate your thinking to view enemies as positive forces in your life, because:

Enemies make you better. They fill you with purpose and direction. Enemies don't permit you to rest on your laurels or get too comfortable. They keep your edge from dulling, constantly reminding you to sharpen the business side of the blade. You're only as good as your strongest enemy.

Enemies are symbols. Conflict is an invisible force, but an enemy is a palpable entity. You can see and hear an enemy; they adhere to physical properties of nature. People are fearful of what they can't tangibly observe. That's why a conflict concept such as terrorism is so unsettling and terrifying. It's an imperceptible, wraithlike agent of violence with no discernible form. This is why the US government selected a specific symbol in the form of Osama bin Laden to represent the overarching threat of "terrorism" in general. It gave the United States a bull's-eye. Unfortunately, when you cut the head off that kind of snake, another one grows right back in its place. While it's nearly impossible to fight a vapor, naming an enemy gives you something concrete to target.

Enemies create controversy. It's always nice to have someone else telling people that you're nuts. Controversy, artfully directed, can lead to some exceptionally powerful outcomes. Having someone else create controversy around you is a way to position yourself and stand out beyond the masses of asses.

Enemies send social proofing signals. Having enemies

is a signal to others that you're worth the price of admission. People will be compelled to pay attention to you since someone else worthwhile is paying attention to you, even if it's negative. Especially if it's negative.

Enemies are fun. Life is a game. A game we take seriously, but a game nonetheless. It's no fun playing against yourself. (Playing *with* yourself is a different story.) You want someone on the other side of the net to hit the ball back. Bobby Fischer can only play both sides of the board so many times before he starts to go crazy.

The only thing more important than *having* enemies is *casting* your enemies.

Like any great Bond movie, it all comes down to casting (suck it, George Lazenby).

As such, you need to cast enemies worthy of your aspirations. What do I mean by that? Babe Ruth didn't step up to the plate and point his bat at first base, did he? No, he pointed to the fucking outfield bleachers like a boss, because Babe Ruth wasn't about hitting doubles. He was about hitting home runs. As should you. Think like the Babe and aim for someone in a position of power, a position you eventually want to be in, to cast as your enemy. By calling out the guy sitting in the seat you want to be in, attaching your name to his, you subconsciously proclaim to the universe that you're on the same level. You've jumped a few perception rungs on the ladder simply by talking shit.

It's like when a newbie prize fighter wins one fight and starts lipping off in the post-bout interview about coming after the reigning champ. He's setting his sights high and letting the world know that his target is the guy wearing the gold belt. Not the chump he has to fight next, or the twenty other clowns in line after him; his eyes are on the mountain's summit, not all the rocks he has to climb over to get to it. All of a sudden he's not perceived as the lowly newcomer who's won one fight; he's the rising star exhibiting mad promise challenging the big dog to a showdown.

Casting the right enemy can also result in unexpected reversals of fortune.

One morning, years ago—as I was covertly poaching agents and clients all over town to set up my new agency—I got a call from Barbara "Babs" Miller, my ex-boss, Terrance's ex-wife, and a powerful agent in her own regard. She wanted to have lunch. Initially, I turned her down as I had more important things to do in my plot to ambush the entertainment world, but she was insistent, dropping not-so-subtle-hints that she knew what I was up to and it would be in my best interest to sit down with her.

I begrudgingly agreed.

It wasn't until I got to the restaurant of her choosing that I realized *I* was the one getting ambushed. Sitting at a table in the back room was Babs, along with the head of every major agency in Hollywood, waiting for me and catching me completely off guard. Everyone was in attendance. A modern-day meeting of the Five Families. That bastard Terrance from my old firm, TMA, was there, along with representatives from CAA, ICM, William Morris, Endeavor, and, laughingly, APA.

I was down, but I wasn't out. The benefits of a surprise

attack are fleeting, and—like how our brave American soldiers responded quickly to ward off a third-wave bombing by the Japanese at Pearl Harbor—I, too, summoned all my faculties to rally against the immediate threat at hand. With only a flicker of hesitation, I put a mile-wide smile on my face and sat down at the table as if I had invited all these fuckstains to afternoon tea. It was an unfair fight, but you don't always get to make the odds.

I turned to Babs and said loud enough so only she could hear, "I knew that you liked dick, Babs. I just didn't know you were a cocksucker."

Terrance sat at the head of table, looking at me with a twinkle in his eye and that smug little grin he flashed occasionally to let people know he had bested them. He let the gravity of the moment settle, then said, "Ari, the seven of us who represent most of the power in this town are lined up to say, if you go near one of our clients or one of our agents or even one of our highly prized mailroom boys, we will all come down on you with the wrath of ten thousand suns." Say what you will about the man (God knows I've said plenty), he was a brilliant tactician and a formidable opponent; he knew how to hit you where it hurt. For all intents and purposes, the new Gold Agency was about to be out of business before it even opened.

As I sat there, doing a Terminator-style analysis of everyone at the table, scanning for any entry points of weakness, a thought occurred to me: What happens when an alpha male shark gets injured? The smaller sharks around him see opportunity, gang up, and—one by one—take progressively larger bites out of him until he's a floating carcass.

The enemy of those *in* power are those who *want* power.

Terrance, by far, had the most juice in the room. He was the alpha shark; everyone else, the smaller sharks. I knew what I had to do. I had to cast my enemy. And I'd just found the right Ensure-drinking, shriveled-up asshole for the role.

In a game of tennis, you can hit the ball to the left, you can hit the ball to the right, or you can hit the ball over your opponent. But there's also a fourth option. You can hit the ball directly *through* them. I've always been a fan of responding head-on, so, instead of denying or dodging, I admitted to the room that, yes, the rumors were true—I was starting a new agency. Amid their exclamations of temporary victory at my confirmation I added, "Ari Gold is back and gonna be bigger than ever. But I assure you, and I swear this on my children's names, I have no intention of going after any of your clients." Then, in one of my most masterful moves ever, I pointed right at Terrance and said, "Only *his*." The shock of this singularly pointed declaration of war was audible. Gasps all around. The color in Terrance's face drained. By letting the room know that (1) I was back and wasn't going anywhere and (2) I was going after Terrance's business and only Terrance's business, I not only reduced my enemy count from seven to one, I dropped a nuclear bomb that broke up their makeshift alliance and gave every other agency clearance to join me and go after Terrance, as well.

What do smaller sharks do when a bigger shark is injured? They get out their silverware, throw on a bib, and fucking feast.

I ultimately had to partner up with Barbara, the traitorous bitch who exposed me in the first place, to get the funds necessary to start what would become the now infamous Miller/Gold Agency, but that was a small concession on the campaign trail to victory, and in the end she turned out to be a strong ally. The strategy worked, and it wasn't too much later, with the help of the other agencies, that I was able to drive Terrance out of the business entirely.

Find an enemy worthy of your aspirations and set phasers to Kill.

Once you have them in your sights, type in the launch codes and go *Judgment Day* on their ass.

To be successful you need friends. To be very successful you need enemies.

RULE #18

Never Let 'Em Forget You're the Baddest Motherfucker in the Room

"What I'm capable of doing and what you're capable of doing are two totally different things."

We've arrived at our final rule. Number 18. Why eighteen? I've got hundreds more, but need to get on to my next project, so fuck you. Regardless, all the prior rules lead to this one: your legend.

If you've actually been paying attention and following any of these rules, stories of your heroism will be passed from town to town, elevating you to superhuman status and cementing both your position and your power. Jerry Weintraub signed Elvis in Vegas by bringing the King a million bucks in a briefcase. Kathryn Bigelow may or may not have shot bin Laden herself in order to shape the storyline of *Zero Dark Thirty*. Jimmy Caan plowed twenty-three straight months of *Playboy* cover girls on a dare.

Legends are created when bold action is taken, when power

is asserted in emphatic and creative ways, and when your greatness reminds your subjects that you are the baddest motherfucker in the room.

In September 2009, my old mentor, Terrance McQuewick, walked into my office at Miller/Gold and offered to sell me his company, TMA, for $100 million. This was my former idol, the man who groomed me for greatness and later betrayed me in spectacular fashion, now dangling the keys to his castle three feet from the script for *Extremely Fast and Incredibly Furious*. This was Darth Vader offering Luke the keys to the Death Star, Warren Buffett selling Berkshire Hathaway to Bill Gates, or Barbara Walters handing her plastic surgeon's contact information to Katie Couric.

As I mentioned earlier in this book, TMA was filled with my peers, friends, and enemies. I popped my millionaire cherry at TMA on my way to building that agency into a Hollywood powerhouse. TMA was also the location of my lowest professional moment, when Terrance, in a fit of jealousy, fired me in front of the entire company. None of the sheep in that office were willing to risk their own security by standing up for me, so naturally I was intrigued by the possibility of purchasing and subsequently shearing their professional careers. For the right price.

As it turned out, Terrance had been caught cheating on his fourth wife with their daughter's Bar Method instructor and was about to go through a messy divorce. He had to sell his company quickly and quietly in order to avoid having it carved up in his domestic dispute, which is why I was eventually able to buy TMA at a twenty-five percent discount. The entire negotiation took less time than it took me to chart the ideal course for my vengeance.

There have been many legendary acts of redemption and revenge throughout the ages, from Hammurabi to the Forty-seven Ronin and Aaron Burr, but none were quite as satisfying, humiliating, or emphatic as when I stepped off the elevator into the TMA offices with an ax to grind and a semiautomatic paintball gun to unload.

Over the next ten minutes I stormed that building like the beaches of Normandy, annihilating every disloyal agent in that office, along with most of the reality TV department. I was a god, determining who lived and died with every slight hitch of my trigger finger. My Terminator rampage was unlike anything Hollywood had ever seen, and I made sure to leave some survivors so that they could tell the rest of the town of my greatness and audacity. While punishing all the leftover Benedict Arnolds in Terrance's colony, I was simultaneously sending a powerful message: Stay loyal to Ari Gold and you will prosper. Cross him and you will die a death worse than a thousand hells.

Fittingly, the last person to feel the sting of my steel was Adam Davies, the agent who first sold me out to Terrance those precious few years earlier. In another life, Davies could have been my successor. He certainly possessed the raw intellect, charisma, and business savvy to carry the torch, but, alas, he never had the balls. Davies was a born henchman, destined to operate in the shadows behind his master, in this case an aging Brit with Tiger Woods's taste for value-meal mistresses. *Does it really have to end like this*, I thought momentarily as I pumped round after round into Davies's designer suit, effectively transforming the guy into a champagne room couch. Of course it fucking did. Insubordination must be stomped out like the hardwood floors at Kappa Alpha Psi.

As Adam Davies walked through the hallways of TMA humiliated and blacklisted, he surely regretted his insolence. And when a video of Davies's shameful stroll made its way onto the Internet, the rest of Hollywood got the opportunity to relearn what they should have already known: Ari Gold will always be the baddest motherfucker in the room.

■ GOLD NUGGET ■
THE FINAL GOLD NUGGET

You will never be me.

You can memorize this book. Study every move I've ever made. Tattoo my rules down your spine.

But memorization is different than knowing. Studying isn't the same thing as doing. And tattoos are something teenage girls get when their dad won't let them date a guy who calls himself DJ Centipede.

Only I have the Midas touch. Only I was kissed by the sun. My name isn't Ari Bronze. It isn't Ari Silver. It's Ari Motherfucking Gold. And like the Highlander, there can be only one.

You will never be *me*.

But that doesn't mean you shouldn't try.

You were smart enough to pick up this book, so you're off to a strong start. But just because you read the Bible don't make you the pope. If you fail, that's not on me, just destiny closing the loop on the belly flop that is your life. Those of you who succeed in the world will be in my debt forever. Make sure you act like it. Who knows, one day I may come to collect...

As my final gold nugget, I leave you with this:

While each and every one of you should kiss my golden ass for sharing these insights with you, no hard-and-fast set of rules will ever guarantee you the crown. In the end, when it comes to rules, you have to do as I have done: Go out and make your fucking own.

And if you ever wake up feeling bold, and want to take a shot at the king, I'll be waiting.

Until then,

STAY GOLD.

ACKNOWLEDGMENTS

The author would like to thank Doug Ellin, Joey Boukadakis, and Jake Greene for their assistance in the creation of this book. It literally could not have been done without them.

ABOUT THE AUTHOR

Power agent Ari Gold received his undergraduate degree from Harvard University before earning his JD/MBA at the University of Michigan. He is the co-founder, former senior partner, and co-CEO of Miller/Gold Talent Agency and the former owner of Terrance McQuewick Agency, where he represented a long roster of A-list celebrities. He lives in Los Angeles with his wife and two children.

PHOTO CREDITS